HELENNA SNOWDEN

Yes, You Can Start a Small Business in Texas

Your Easy Step-by-Step Guide

First edition

ISBN: 979-8-234-01350-7

This book was professionally typeset on Reedsy.
Find out more at reedsy.com

To my fellow market vendors who inspired me to share what I've learned. May you be joyful and successful in all your endeavors.

To my sister for being my first reader
To my mom for passing down her love of plants
To my husband for supporting me through all my projects

Contents

Introduction

This book is for anyone in Texas who has a business idea and hasn't yet taken action. If you've been dreaming of starting your bakery or your jewelry business but you just don't know how to make it official, this book is for you. If you've started selling products but haven't looked into the paperwork, this book is for you.

I've started several businesses, both LLCs and Sole Proprietorships, so I know the process. The process can be confusing and it requires a lot of research and reading. Since that is something I enjoy doing, I decided to write it all down in a book. I'll explain what paperwork you need and how to fill it out. I'll go over the process of filing income tax and sales tax. I'll also explain how to track sales and spending and share my tracking spreadsheet with you. I'll give you tips for naming your business and ideas for figuring out where to sell. By the end of this book, you'll feel confident and inspired to make your business official.

So if you're ready to jump in and get started, now is the time! Just follow the steps I've outlined in Section I to learn how to set up your business, then move on to Section II to learn about business administration, and finally Section III to learn how to sell your products. I've also added occasional sections for your own notes, as well as helpful links and a spreadsheet you can use to track your revenue. Good luck and I wish you a fun and successful business journey!

I

Registering Your Small Business

1

Step 1: Choose Your Business Name

N aming your business is one of the best parts of starting a business. It's a chance to tell the world what you want them to think about your work. It's a way to express yourself and create something new of your very own.

Using Your Own Name

You can do business as yourself if you don't need a separate name for your business. For example, if your business is dog sitting, maybe you post your services on your city's Facebook pages using your personal Facebook account. If your name is Jessica Jackson and you offer dog sitting, then people will just contact you, Jessica Jackson, for dog sitting. In this case you won't have a separate business name.

When you use your own name as your business name, you can shift the focus of your business as it suits you. If you want to start a business baking cookies and later decide to sell home-cooked dinners instead, your business name still fits. Using your own name also means that you won't need to register an assumed name for your business, but more about that later. Registering an assumed name isn't difficult, so don't let that stop you either way.

Chances are, your name is unique and will stand out among other businesses. This is a good thing, because you want people to remember you so that they can buy from you again.

Using your name can also be helpful if you plan to post on social media, since you will be able to use the accounts you already have. If you name your business something different, it will make more sense to create new social media accounts for that name.

A potential downside of using your name is that it will not tell your potential customers what your business does. You will have to explain to them what you do and why they should purchase from you.

If you have an unusual name, it can also be hard for people to spell or remember, which can hurt your business. You want people to know your name and come back again and again. If you have a common name, someone may already be using it for their own business and people may get confused if you do business in the same area.

Another option is combining your name with the type of item or service you offer. For example, you can choose something like "Jessica Jackson Pet Sitting" or "Sara's Sourdough". This will give you more options while still using your name. You can also use just your first name or just your last name, it's up to you. Just be aware that even if you use your name plus a word that is not part of your name, you will need to register it as an assumed name.

Creating a Unique Business Name

If you decide not to use your own name as your business name, you have a lot of options. While it may seem overwhelming, choosing a business name doesn't have to be scary. You can use a few different methods to help you, but often a shorter name is better, and so is a name that explains what your business does.

A quick way to get some ideas is to ask an AI like Chat GPT. You can describe your business and ask for name suggestions. Write down the ones you like, on actual paper preferably. Ask the AI to tweak things, or use certain words. Think about what you want people to feel when they hear your business name. Should they feel confident, joyful, or excited to hear about your business? Do you want a funny name, or a professional name? What kind of person do you hope to serve with your business, and what kind of name would this person be drawn to?

One of my favorite ways to name a business is to write a list. Get out a piece of paper and start writing down every descriptive word that comes to mind when you think about your business. For example, if you are a baker, write down words like "sweet, fresh, tasty, hot, yummy, delicious, chocolate, oven, flour, spices, baker, cupcakes" etc. Some words will come to mind, and you'll immediately realize they won't work, but write them down anyway. Otherwise, you will just keep getting stuck on them. Write down all the words that come to mind. Think about what you want customers to think when they see your products or experience your services.

Next, start circling the words you like or that stand out to you. Cross out words you don't like. Start combining words and writing them down. See what looks and sounds good. Maybe "Flour and Chocolate" or "The Weekend Baker" sounds good to you. Maybe you like "Tanya's Fresh Bakes" or "Sweets and Spices Bakery". The final name is up to you, but it can help to get friends and family to weigh in, too. They might see something you don't.

If you want to be able to abbreviate your business name down to its initials, make sure it doesn't spell out anything silly or offensive. You don't want to realize this after you've already ordered your signs or made your website.

Finally, take some time. You don't have to name your business in one day. Write your list and set it aside. Look at it again a few days later. Show it to a few people. Sleep on it. Try a few names out loud. How do you feel about telling people your business name?

Once you have some ideas, a great way to finalize your business name is with a thesaurus or Google search. If you have a name you like, but you aren't 100% sure, put some of the words through a thesaurus and see if there is a synonym that you like better. If you want your business name to rhyme but it doesn't, maybe a synonym will. Or try doing a google search for words that rhyme with your chosen word. If your name has a color in it, a thesaurus can find great alternatives. For example, you can use "crimson" instead of "red", or "plum" instead of "purple". Be as creative as you'd like!

Anything you'd like to write down?

How to Check Whether a Name is in Use

You have a few options if you want to see if someone is already using the business name you've chosen. But luckily, you only need to check this if you are forming an LLC. That's because Sole Proprietorships are allowed to have the same name as another Sole Proprietorship. Don't worry, I'll explain the difference between an LLC and a Sole Proprietorship in a later chapter.

If you later want to form an LLC, it is a good idea to do this search at that time, since the Secretary of State will not register another LLC with the same name. You don't need to check names in other states since it won't affect your registration. While you can check now, by the time you decide to register an LLC, someone could have taken your chosen name.

Do a domain search

You can do a domain search to see if someone owns the domain name. If they do, chances are a business with that name exists. The way to check this is to go to a domain marketplace like **Namecheap.com** or **GoDaddy.com** and perform a search for the name. The site will tell you if the domain is taken. If you don't know what a domain is, it is the part of a website between the "www." and the ".com" for the main page of the site.

When you search a domain name on a domain sales site like those I mentioned, you will also be given alternative similar names. This can be another way to come up with good names for your business. This is the easiest way to check, but it won't check for Texas specifically, so you may think a name is taken, when actually it is available in Texas.

Do a Secretary of State search

You can also check with the Texas Secretary of State to see if a business name is registered. This will only check businesses registered as entities other than Sole Proprietorships, because Sole Proprietorships are not registered through the secretary of state, they are registered locally (more on that later). You can email the Texas Secretary of State at **corpinfo@sos.texas.gov** to ask if a business name is registered. You can also call (512) 463-5555 to find out if a name is being used by a registered business.

Another option is to use their online system at **direct.sos.state.tx.us/acc t/acct-login.asp**, but you will need to create an account and pay one dollar per name search. When you log in, you will be asked to verify a credit card or use your client account funds. Once you are logged in, click on "Business Organization" at the top of the page. Then under the section "Inquiries and Orders" click on "Name Availability Search".

This will cost $1 and tell you, as stated on the website, whether or not "the name you propose to use is currently in use, reserved, or registered by a corporation, limited liability company, or limited partnership filed with the secretary of state." Notice that it does not tell you if your proposed name is being used by a Sole Proprietorship.

What if I can't or don't want to choose a name yet?

It's ok! Start your business anyway. Just use your own name without any additions and change it later. The best time to start your business is now! The longer you wait until you're ready or until everything is perfect, the more likely you are to never start at all.

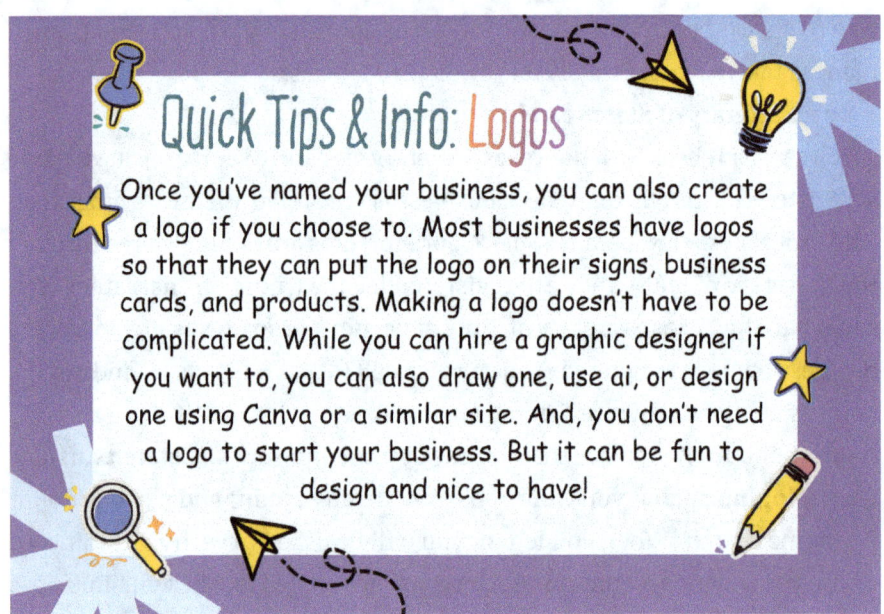

Quick Tips & Info: Logos

Once you've named your business, you can also create a logo if you choose to. Most businesses have logos so that they can put the logo on their signs, business cards, and products. Making a logo doesn't have to be complicated. While you can hire a graphic designer if you want to, you can also draw one, use ai, or design one using Canva or a similar site. And, you don't need a logo to start your business. But it can be fun to design and nice to have!

2

Step 2: Choose Your Business Entity

For a small business just starting out, you have two main options: a Limited Liability Company or a Sole Proprietorship. The default is the Sole Proprietorship. That means that if you don't make a decision, you will be doing business as a Sole Proprietorship automatically.

You may be wondering if you can start as a Sole Proprietorship and later become an Limited Liability Company (LLC), and the answer is yes, you can. In most cases you won't even need to change your business' name as long as no other registered business is using it. Since there is no cost associated with starting a Sole Proprietorship, some businesses do choose to start there and then form an LLC later on once they have earned enough money to pay for LLC registration.

Sole Proprietorship

When you start doing business, the default business entity is a Sole Proprietorship. A Sole Proprietorship has one member, and that's you, the Sole Proprietor. All business earnings are treated as your personal income and are recorded on Schedule C of your income tax return, as are all losses.

With a Sole Proprietorship, you and your business are treated as one. That means your business' liability is your liability, and your assets are at risk if your business is ever sued. But there are still options you can set up to protect you, like business liability insurance (more on this later).

A Sole Proprietorship also doesn't register a business name for you. It assumes that you will use your own name for your business unless you register an assumed name certificate with your county clerk.

If you want to start a business together with someone else and don't file for a specific entity, you'll be starting a general partnership, which is the default for two or more people who start a business together. The profits and losses will be split and filed by each member on their own tax return. All partners can be liable for any other partner's actions.

Because there is nothing that you need to do in order to form a Sole Proprietorship, it is the fastest way to form a business. But it also offers you the least liability protection.

Limited Liability Company

The other common way to set up a small business is by forming an LLC. A Limited Liability Company (LLC) has the goal of reducing your liability by creating a separation between you and your business. If you form an LLC, it is your job to preserve this separation by keeping business and personal finances completely separate. You also need to keep records of meetings and LLC decisions. Otherwise, you could lose your liability protection if someone were to sue you. But when done correctly, only the assets belonging to the LLC are at risk and your personal assets are safe.

To set up an LLC in Texas, you need to file a Certificate of Formation with the Texas Secretary of State and pay a filing fee of $300. You also need to write and sign an operating agreement. Your operating agreement explains the rules of your LLC, and who the owners are. The owners of an LLC are known as members.

Your operating agreement also explains how you are funding your LLC. You can fund your LLC with a starting amount of your choosing. If your LLC needs more funds later on, you can add contribute additional amounts as long as you document it properly.

Taxes for single-member LLCs are filed using Schedule C on your personal tax return, as with a Sole Proprietorship. If your LLC has multiple members, you will instead file form 1065 and Schedule K-1 with your personal tax return. You also have the option of filing as a C Corporation or an S Corporation, but these are most common for businesses that have very high earnings. However, I will go over S Corps briefly int the Tax chapter of this book.

Finally, every LLC is required to have something called a 'registered agent'. Your registered agent is on record with the Secretary of State and receives tax and legal documents on behalf of your LLC. You can be your own registered agent, but most LLCs choose to use a registered agent service that fills this roll. This protects your privacy, because the address of your registered agent will be made available publicly. In addition, the registered agent has to be available during business hours. You can easily find and hire a registered agent online, generally for $100 or less per year.

While the initial setup can sound complicated, there are pre-written operating agreements that you just need to edit to fit your situation. You can also find printable versions of meeting minutes and other documents, which makes the process a lot easier than it might seem. So don't let the initial set-up scare you away from forming an LLC.

Read the next chapter to learn how to set up your LLC. If you've decided not to set up an LLC at this time, you can skip to Chapter 4 Step 3: Registering an Assumed Name.

Quick Tips & Info: Sole Proprietorship vs LLC

Sole Proprietorship:
- Owners are personally liable for business debts and obligations.
- Income is taxed on the owner's personal tax return.
- Default business entity with no paperwork required.
- Owned and managed by the sole proprietor directly.

Limited Liability Company:
- Owners have limited liability, personal assets are protected.
- Income is taxed on the owner's personal tax return; can choose corporate taxation if desired.
- More complex; requires filing Articles of Organization and fees.
- Can be managed by members or appointed managers.

How to Choose

The biggest differences between a Sole Proprietorship and an LLC are the initial setup cost, potential ongoing costs, and liability protection. Depending on your business, you might not have a lot of liability and a Sole Proprietorship might be all you need. Or, if you are just starting out, you might want to run your business as a Sole Proprietorship for a while before spending the $300 needed to form an LLC.

It is completely fine to wait and form an LLC later on. But if you know you will be sticking with your business and you want the best protection, an LLC is the way to go. Having those three letters at the end of your business name also makes your business look more legitimate and professional. And when you set up your business banking, some banks will only accept LLCs or other registered entities. If you aren't sure, reading the next chapter about the formation process of an LLC might help you decide.

If the prospect of forming an LLC is stopping you, then starting with a Sole Proprietorship is a perfectly reasonable option. You don't need to rush into forming an LLC if you just want to get the basics set up so you can start selling.

My NoTes:

What are your thoughts? What do you think will work better for you, Sole Proprietorship or LLC? Or would you rather read more about the set up process before you decide?

3

Step 2b: Forming an LLC

Y ou have two options when forming your LLC. You can complete the process yourself, or you can have a service do it for you. Both are good options, but it is usually cheaper to do it yourself. I'm going to explain everything step-by-step so that you can set up your LLC on your own, but I'll also explain what most services offer and what they charge, so you can decide what the best option is for you.

Your LLC can be a single-member LLC, meaning you are the only member, or it can have multiple members. A single-member LLC is the easiest to manage and file taxes for. The exception is if you are married and your spouse is a member of your LLC. In that case, your LLC will still be treated as a single-member LLC for tax purposes. While you can have additional members, you can also hire employees if you need help. You don't need to make someone a member of your LLC in order to use their services. And, if you are the only member, all the decisions are yours alone, giving you more control.

Setting up and managing an LLC involves 4 steps

- **Step 1:** Choose a registered agent to receive legal and tax documents on your LLC's behalf.
- **Step 2:** File certificate of formation with the Texas Secretary of State to create your LLC

- **Step 3:** Create and sign your operating agreement
- **Step 4:** Maintain your LLC keeping separate finances, filing franchise reports, etc

LLC Set Up Services

An LLC set up service will make sure that your LLC name is available and will file your Certificate of Formation. Some will also create your operating agreement, act as your registered agent, include a domain name, website, phone service, email, or other services. You'll usually need to pay a set-up fee in addition to the $300 LLC filing fee charged by the Texas Secretary of State. Below I will go over some options you can choose and their pricing and offers. You can also find other options, but these are some of the ones you are likely to find when looking for a set up service.

Legal Zoom is a well-known service for a variety of legal matter. They will file your Certificate of Formation with the Secretary of State for free and you'll just pay the $300 filing fee. They also give you the option of scheduling a phone consultation with a tax accountant. Just be careful if you accept the tax consultation because they may try to sign you up for accounting services for a fee.

Their next tier of service costs $249 + state filing fees and includes everything in the free service as well as the creation of your operating agreement, which sets up the rules for your LLC and is required. They'll also apply for your an EIN and provide you with a website through Wix. In addition, you get access to attorney consults and editable document templates for a limited time, along with a few other perks.

Their premium version costs $299 and includes bookkeeping, mileage tracking, and customizable proposals and documents. You can compare the options on their site here **legalzoom.com/business/business-formation/l lc-overview.html**. Note that *Legal Zoom* does not include registered agent services, so you would need to set that up separately.

Bizee offers similar options, but their free tier (+ filing fee of course) offers a year of registered agent service in addition to filing your articles of incorporation (another name for the Certificate of Formation). Their next step up, for $199 + filing fees, includes everything in the free plant, plus the operating agreement, EIN, and a domain name and business email. Their premium version adds a business phone number and document templates, as well as expedited filing for $299. Find a comparison of their options here **orders.bizee.com/form-order-now.php**. You'll just need to input your state to view the correct pricing. After the first year, their registered agent services are $119 annually.

A third option is **northwestregisteredagent.com/llc**. They can file your Certificate of Formation, create your operating agreement, and be your registered agent, all for just $39 plus filing fees. After that, registered agent services are $125 per year, but it does include a domain, website, email, and phone number. They can also file your franchise tax report for $100 per year, although this is easy to do yourself. *Northwest Registered Agent* is a good choice if you want ongoing perks like a website, domain, and more.

Finally, there is **texasregisteredagent.net/form-an-llc** which charges $135 to form your LLC and then just $35 annually for registered agent fees. They will also create your operating agreement and provide a domain name as well as email and phone service. This is a great option since your recurring charges will be low. But if you prefer one of the other set up services, you can always choose *Texas Registered Agent* solely as your registered agent once your LLC has been established.

If you choose one of these options and it does not include an operating agreement, you can easily use an online template. You will need to create a login and username, but you'll be able to create your operating agreement for free. Some options are **rocketlawyer.com/sem/llc-operating-agreement**, legal templates at **legaltemplates.net/form/llc-operating-agreement**, docusign templates at **docusign.com/templates/llc-operating-agreement**, and templates from Northwest Registered Agent at **northwestregisteredagent.com/llc/texas/operating-agreement**.

If they ask you to sign up for a free trial before letting you download your operating agreement, make sure you put a cancellation date in your calendar so that you remember to cancel before you get charged. These websites are the same ones I recommend you use if you are doing the entire process yourself. It is much easier than writing out the operating agreement manually, and much more likely to include all the required items.

Before creating an operating agreement, you need to know who your registered agent will be, and a few details about how you want your LLC to be set up. So before you jump in, please read the sections on registered agents and operating agreements, even if you plan to use an LLC set up service.

While using a set up service can be convenient, I do want to make one important point before you decide. The downside of set up services, even the affordable ones, is that you lose out on the experience of setting up your own LLC. Because of that, it will be harder for you to make changes to your LLC since you won't have the knowledge of how the process works or how to use the Secretary of State website. You will need to ask your set up service to make changes for you, such as changing the name of your LLC or registering an assumed name, or you will need to create your Secretary of State online account so that you can do it yourself.

Set Up Services and Registered Agents:

- **legalzoom.com/business/business-formation/llc-overview.html** from free-$299, no registered agent service
- **orders.bizee.com/form-order-now.php** from free-$299, then $119 annually for registered agent
- **northwestregisteredagent.com/llc** $39, then $125 annually for registered agent + domain, website, email, phone
- **texasregisteredagent.net/form-an-llc** $135, then $35 annually for registered agent

Operating Agreement Options:

- **rocketlawyer.com/sem/llc-operating-agreement**
- **legaltemplates.net/form/llc-operating-agreement**
- **docusign.com/templates/llc-operating-agreement**

· **northwestregisteredagent.com/llc/texas/operating-agreement**.

Step 1: Choose Your Registered Agent

Before you can file your Certificate of Formation and create your operating agreement, you need a registered agent. You will be asked to list them on both your Certificate of Formation and your operating agreement.

Your registered agent is required to be available to receive tax and legal mail during business hours. Their address will also be public record. Your registered agent will send you a scan of your important mail. Some will also forward you physical mail.. Some will scan and send you non-urgent mail as well, such as mail from clients or other people who find the address, but most will only forward necessary mail to you.

You are allowed to act as your LLC's registered agent, but it is usually better to hire a service to do this for you. That's because someone has to be physically available at the listed address during business hours. Otherwise, you are not meeting the requirements of the state of Texas. In addition, most people don't want their private address to be available publicly, which is what happens to the address you list as your registered agent. You also cannot get around this by using a PO box as your registered agent address since a person associated with your LLC is supposed to be available.

You may be wondering how often you will receive mail through your registered agent. Most likely, it won't be frequent at all. But the important thing is to have one when you need it. And you cannot start an LLC without one.

You can easily sign up for a registered agent service online. They will tell you what address to use when you file your LLC. They can also file franchise tax for you, but they will charge for that and probably ask you for information in order to do so, which means it is easier and cheaper to just do it yourself. Don't worry, it is very simple and I will go over how to do this later.

Some registered agents you can use are *Bizee* at **bizee.com/business-mana gement/registered-agent**, which charges $119 per year. *Northwest Registered Agent* charges $125 per year and includes a domain, website, email, and phone number for your business. *Texas Registered Agent* charges only $35 per year and also gives you a domain. *True Texas Registered Agent* charges $44 per year and can forward physical mail to you if you request it. You can look into these options and choose the best one, or find a registered agent online by doing your own search. Just compare their offerings and pricing to see what works best for you.

How to Change Your Registered Agent

You are allowed to change registered agent. You just need to notify the Secretary of State using their online system, and of course inform your current and future registered agent. Some registered agents will also submit your change request for you. To file online using the Secretary of State website, you will need the information from your Certificate of Formation, so you can only change your registered agent after your LLC is set up.

At that point, just go to **sos.state.tx.us/corp/sosda/index.shtmland** log into the Secretary of State website. Once logged in, choose and agree to pay either by credit card or by funding your online account.

Then, select "Business Organizations" at the top. Look for the section labeled "Web Filings" and then type the filing number for your LLC into the field under "Change Document". You can find your filing number on your certificate of filing that you received from the Secretary of State when you filed your Certificate of Formation. You can also find it in the top right corner of your Certificate of Formation. After you have entered the number, click "File Document". On the next screen, you'll be able to select "Change of Registered Agent/Office" from the drop down and complete the filing.

In addition, you should update your operating agreement with an amendment saying who your new registered agent is. You can use an online template like this one **legaltemplates.net/form/llc-operating-agreement/amendment** or this one **eforms.com/operating-agreements/amendment**. You will just need to create a free account on the website and download, save, and also print your amendment.

Step 2: File Your Certificate of Formation

Now that you have a registered agent, it's time to make your LLC official! Make sure you are on the correct website before you start. Many LLC set up services will show up on Google before the Secretary of State website does. You don't want to accidentally complete paperwork on the wrong website because they will either charge you, or you'll have to fill everything out a second time.

The Certificate of Formation, sometimes called the Articles of Organization, is what you file with the Secretary of State to create your LLC. The Certificate of Formation is a form you fill out with your LLC's name, address, member names, and registered agent. After you submit, the Secretary of State will issue you a Certificate of Filing, which tells you that your Certificate of Formation was received and found to be in order. This means your LLC has been created. You should keep both documents in your files. You will need to refer to them if you want to make any changes to your LLC.

To file your Certificate of Formation online, you need to create an account with the Secretary of State. Go to **direct.sos.state.tx.us/acct/acct-subscribe .asp** and fill out the information with either your info or your business info. Either option is ok, but I would use your info just in case your business name turns out not to be available. That way you won't have an account named after a business that doesn't exist.

After your account is created, you will be able to log in at **direct.sos.state.tx. us/acct/acct-login.asp** and you'll be asked to provide credit card information to complete the login. This is a standard part of the process and you'll have to complete this if you want to file online. You can also select the "client account" option instead of the "credit card" option. This allows you to add funds to your account that you can use later.

Next, click "continue" at the top. On the next page, select "Business Organizations". Under "Inquiries and Orders" select "Name Availability Search". This search will cost $1 to complete, but it's important to make sure that your business name is available before you file. Enter the complete name as you want it to appear, and include "LLC, L.L.C, or Limited Liability Company" at the end, whichever way you prefer. Click "Search" to see if your name is available.

Click again on "Business Organizations" at the top of the screen, then find the section titled "Reservation Formation Registration Documents". From the drop-down, select "Domestic Limited Liability Company (LLC)" and click "File Document".

On the next screen, select "Certificate of Formation" from the drop-down. It should be the only option available. Click "Continue" and follow the prompts.

One of the questions you will be asked is whether you are creating a Professional Limited Liability Company or a General-Purpose Limited Liability Company. In most cases, you should select the "general-purpose" option. The Professional option is only if you will be providing a service that requires licensing, such as a lawyer or a doctor.

You will also be asked to enter your registered agent's information and confirm that they have consented to take on this role. Do not enter the name of your LLC here, as the LLC cannot be its own registered agent. If you want to be your LLC's registered agent then you would enter your own name.

Another question you will need to answer is how your LLC will be managed. An LLC can be member-managed or manager-managed. A member-managed LLC is managed by the member, or owners, of the LLC. In other words, it's managed by you. A manager-managed LLC is managed by external managers who run the LLC but don't own it. Most likely you will be running your own LLC, so in that case it would be member-managed.

The rest of the form will ask for member's name's and addresses, the business address, and other basic information. Before you can submit your filing, you will also be asked to pay the filing fee of $300. After that, you just need to wait to receive your Certificate of Filing stating that your Certificate of Formation has been accepted. Now your LLC officially exists!

Be sure to keep both a paper and electronic copy of your Certificate of Filing and your Certificate of Formation. If you the site suggests that you print something out for your records, you should do so. Better to print it just in case rather than to need it later and not have it.

Step 3: Create Your Operating Agreement

Your operating agreement is the document that explains how your LLC will operate. It is like your LLC's constitution or bylaws. It will explain how new members can join, how voting will work, who the members are, and how much money each member contributed to start the LLC. While you don't need to contribute a lot, you do need to contribute something as part of the set up process. If you contribute $20 to your LLC when you create it, and another owner contributes $20, you will have 50/50 ownership. If you are the only owner, you will have 100% ownership. An LLC needs a little bit of money to get started.

Even though you don't have to file the operating agreement with the state, you will need it if you are asked to provide documentation for your LLC. For example, banks can ask for your operating agreement when you request a business bank account.

You can make changes to your operating agreement by adding an amendment, so if you aren't sure about all the details, you can still create your operating agreement because it can be edited later. Once you have your operating agreement completed, all members need to sign it, agreeing to abide by its rules.

While you could do the research and type up your operating agreement yourself, it's much easier and faster to use a template. Most of these are free, although they will ask you to create an account before letting you download your completed document. But it is worth it because you will have your operating agreement completed and your LLC ready to go.

You can use the template at **rocketlawyer.com/sem/llc-operating-agreem ent** or **legaltemplates.net/form/llc-operating-agreement. D**ocusign has one as well, at **docusign.com/templates/llc-operating-agreement**, and so does Northwest Registered Agent at **northwestregisteredagent.com/llc/texas/ope rating-agreement**. But feel free to try another website, or even create several drafts and then use the one you like best.

You should sign your operating agreement as a member of the LLC or with your title. For example, you can write "member", "managing member", "CEO", "Founder", "President" or similar after your signature. But you should write something other than just your name, since this helps legitimize your LLC and emphasizes that your LLC is a separate entity from you. This is how you should sign every LLC document.

If you need to make changes to you operating agreement after signing, you can find templates for that at **legaltemplates.net/form/llc-operating-agr eement/amendment, eforms.com/operating-agreements/amendment** or **northwestregisteredagent.com/legal-forms/llc/operating-agreement-am**

endment.

Step 4: Maintaining Your LLC

1.) LLC Documents Folder

Find a folder or a binder, label it with the name of your LLC, and put all your important LLC documents inside. Also save copies in a folder on your computer. This makes it much easier to apply for bank accounts, check important information, or do your taxes.

- Certificate of Formation
- Certificate of Filing
- Operating Agreement
- Registered Agent's Name and Address
- Passwords: Secretary of State login and password; Comptroller WebFile login and password

2.) Always Sign LLC Documents with Your Title

Adding your title to your signatures is important to make it clear that you are signing as an agent of your LLC and not as yourself. This preserve your LLC's liability protection.

3.) Keep Your Finances Separate

Keep your business and personal finances separate. This is really important to maintain the liability protection that comes with an LLC. You need a business bank account and you need to track every time you add money from your personal account or take out money from the business account. You can even just keep track on a piece of paper. Many bank accounts will also help you track this. I will go into more detail on business bank accounts in Section Two of this book.

You can still contribute money to your LLC. This is known as an "Owner Contribution". All you have to do is transfer the money from your personal account to your LLC. That way, it will be recorded in your business account. On top of that, it is a good idea to track owner contributions in a spreadsheet or a page in your binder. You can just write down the date, the amount of the contribution, and the name of the person it came from.

When you take money out of your LLC, that is known as an "Owner Draw". You can take money out of your LLC at specific times of the year, or when you decide to. Just make sure you follow the regulations for owner draws as written in your operating agreement. And as with owner contributions, you should record the date, the amount, and the LLC member that the money went to.

4.) File Franchise Tax every May 15

The franchise tax is a tax owed by businesses that earn more than $2,650,000 per year. Chances are you will never have to pay this tax. Instead, you will need to file Form 05-102, *Public Information Report.* You can file electronically using the Texas Comptrollers WebFile system **security.app.cpa.state.tx.us/public/login.**

This form is easy to fill out and just tells the Comptroller your current address and business information to keep their records updated. After clicking on "Franchise Tax" next to your business name, just select the option that says "File a Public/Ownership Information Report" and complete the information. If you don't see your business listed, you will need to add it.

5.) Keep Your LLC's Address Updated

If you change your business address, report the change to the Texas Comptroller by logging into your WebFile account at **security.app.cpa.state.tx.us/public/login**. Just click on where it says "Franchise Tax" next to your business, and then on the next page select that you want to "Change Franchise Mailing Address". That's it!

6.) Sales and Use Tax

If you sell taxable items, you will need to remit sales and use tax. To remit sales tax, log into the Comptroller WebFile system at **security.app.cpa.state.tx.us/public/login**. Click where it says "Sales and Use Tax" next to your business and fill out the form. When you apply for your sales and use tax permit, the system will tell you how often you need to file and will also email you to remind you. Read the chapter 8 for more details.

☐ Keep LLC Document Folder

☐ Always Sign with Your Title

☐ Keep Finances Separate

☐ File Franchise Tax May 15

☐ Keep LLC Address Updated

☐ Remit Sales and Use Tax
(if applicable)

[For a deeper dive into LLC information beyond what I've covered here, I recommend Nolo's LLC Handbook by Glen Secor.]

Once you have completed these steps, you will have a functioning LLC! If you are the only member, everything stays relatively simple. If there are other members, you may need to have regular meetings and record meeting minutes. You may also need to agree to certain LLC actions by creating and signing consent forms. The book I recommended above will really help you especially if you are not the only member. However, what I have written here will get you set up. But for other questions or details that may come up later, I recommend that you find additional information for your specific situation or contact a lawyer.

4

Step 3: Register an Assumed Name

Read this chapter if any of the following apply:

- *You own a Sole Proprietorship using a name OTHER THAN your own name*
- *You own a Sole Proprietorship using your own name WITH THE ADDITION of any other words*
- *You own an LLC using a name OTHER THAN the name on your Certificate of Formation*

R egistering an assumed name certificate, also known as a DBA (Doing Business As), allows you to use a name for your business other than your own name or the name of your LLC. The process is different for an LLC than for a Sole Proprietorship, so just read the section that is relevant to you. Most sole proprietors will need to complete this step, while it is less common for LLCs.

How to Register an Assumed Name for a Sole Proprietorship

The easiest way to register an assumed name is to go to your county clerk's office and complete the form in person. They will be able to file it immediately. Just let them know you want to file an assumed name certificate for a Sole Proprietorship. They will help you fill out the correct information and will confirm your signature. They will also accept your payment which is usually $25 for filing a document.

While it is possible to file by mail, it's much easier to do it in person. That's because you need the form for the specific county you are registering in, and these forms are not always easy to locate. You cannot use the form from the Secretary of State website when you are filing as a Sole Proprietorship. In addition, the form will usually need to be notarized as well, and online notaries are generally not accepted. When you go in person, the representative will act as the notary. They will also give you a copy for your files.

Assumed name certificates are valid for a maximum of 10 years, and after that you will need to file a new one. If you move or change the name of your business, you will also need to file a new form. There is no form to update the information on an assumed name certificate, you just have to file it again with the new information.

You should file your assumed name certificate in the county your business is located in. If you don't have a place of business, you will need to file in the county or counties you do business in. If your business is based in your home then that would be the county you register with.

Check online to find your county clerk's office and make sure you have all the information you need. You will need to know what you want to name your business, as well as the business address, and how long you want the name to be registered for. Bring some form of ID as well. You don't need to worry about someone else using the same business name since this doesn't matter for an assumed name filing.

How to Register an Assumed Name for an LLC

When you register an LLC, you also give it a name. But if you want to do business under a second name using the same LLC, you will need to register an assumed name. An example would be if you named your LLC "Jane's Kitchen, LLC" but you also want to do business as "Jane's Tasty Cookies, LLC" or "Sugar Cookies and More".

Unlike the name of your LLC, assumed names will be approved even if someone else has already registered it. Also, your assumed name does not need to include "LLC" or a variation of it, but it can if you want it to.

Assumed name certificates for LLCs need to be registered at the state level rather than the county level. The fee is $25 and you can file online or by mail. To file online using the Secretary of State website, just go to **sos.state.tx.us /corp/sosda/index.shtml** and log in. Once logged in, agree to pay either by credit card or by funding your online account.

Then, select 'Business Organizations' at the top. Look for the section labeled 'Web Filings' and then type the filing number for your LLC into the field under 'Change Document'. You can find your filing number on the Certificate of Filing that you received from the Secretary of State when you filed your Certificate of Formation. It will say "File Number: 1245566" right underneath the name of your LLC.

You can also find it in the top right corner of your Certificate of Formation, where it will be listed as "Filing#: 1234567 01/01/2026" underneath "Filed in the Office of the Secretary of State of Texas" (don't enter the date, just the number). After you have entered the number, click 'File Document'. On the next screen, you'll be able to select 'Certificate of Assumed Business Name' from the drop down and complete the form.

If you prefer to file by mail, note that you need to fill out form 503 in duplicate so that they can mail you back a copy. You can print the form at **sos.state.tx.us/corp/forms/503_boc.pdf** and mail it to:

P.O. Box 13697
Austin, Texas 78711-3697

You can also personally deliver the form to:

James Earl Rudder Office Building, 1019 Brazos,
Austin, Texas 78701

You also need to mail form 807 at **webservices.sos.state.tx.us/forms/payment.pdf** with your credit card information if you aren't paying with money order or check. You can also find form 504 for abandoning an assumed name at **sos.state.tx.us/corp/forms/504_boc.pdf** if you no longer need it.

5

Step 4: Get Your EIN

An EIN, short for Employee Identification Number, is like a Social Security Number for your business. It helps protect your privacy when you open business bank accounts or hire employees. Often, you'll be required to have an EIN before a bank will let you request a business bank account. EINs can even help you build a separate credit score for your business. Both LLCs and Sole Proprietorships, as well as other entities, can apply for an EIN.

Applying for an EIN is fast, easy, and free. All you need to do is fill out a form on the IRS website and then print out the EIN page when it is issued to you. Then, put it in your folder of important documents. You should also save a copy to your computer.

To begin, scroll to the bottom of this page **sa.www4.irs.gov/applyein** and click 'Apply for an EIN'. Complete the form and if approved, your EIN will be issued immediately. If there is a problem, you will receive a message with an error code and a phone number to call.

EINs are specific to the type of entity that they were originally requested for. So if you request an EIN for a Sole Proprietorship, you can't use it for an LLC later. But you can request a new EIN for your LLC.

You also can't request more than one EIN for a Sole Proprietorship, because a Sole Proprietorship is associated with you directly. So basically, your EIN will be assigned to your name but also to your business name, and you can only have one. If you decide to close your Sole Proprietorship and create a new one, you need to ask that your EIN information be updated with your new business name. Otherwise, your requests may be denied when you try to open a bank account because the business name you've entered won't match what the IRS has on file. You can do this by calling the IRS at 800-829-4933. Alternatively, you can send the IRS a letter to request that they change the business name associated with your EIN. Just make sure you list the address you used when you applied for the EIN, as well as the EIN itself, previous business name, and current business name. You can mail your letter to the address listed below.

Department of the Treasury
Internal Revenue Service
Austin, TX 73301-0002

To only change the address of the business connected to your EIN, whether for an LLC or a Sole Proprietorship, you can send Form 8822-B **irs.gov/pub/irs-pdf/f8822b.pdf** to the IRS at:

Department of the Treasury
Internal Revenue Service
Austin, TX 73301-0002

If you have any problems with your EIN, aren't sure if you need a new one, or have lost your EIN, you can call 800-829-4933 for help. I have called before, and while there may be a wait, they are friendly and helpful and will even mail you a confirmation of any changes made to your EIN registration.

I recommend that you apply for your EIN even if you aren't sure you'll need it, because it is quick and easy and you will most likely use it eventually. It's nice to have all the basic business registration tasks out of the way, and this is the final step!

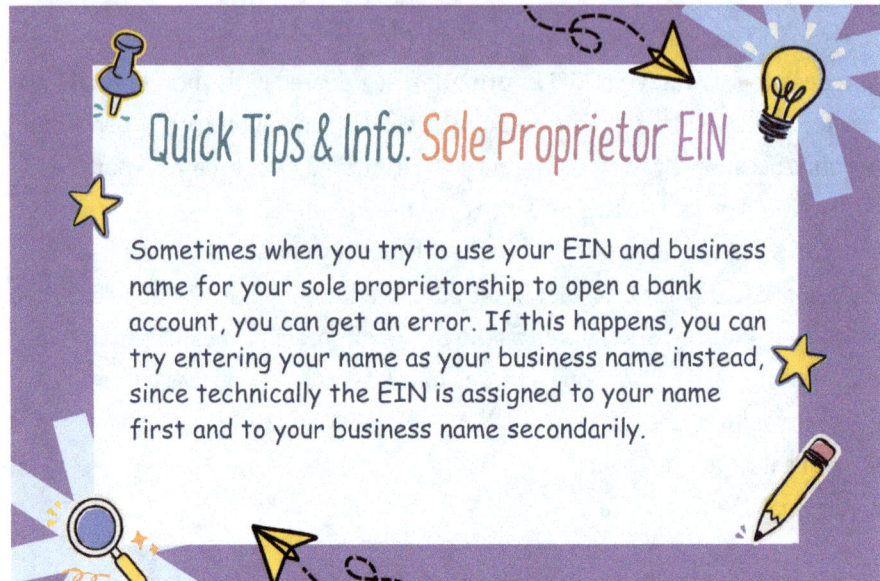

Quick Tips & Info: Sole Proprietor EIN

Sometimes when you try to use your EIN and business name for your sole proprietorship to open a bank account, you can get an error. If this happens, you can try entering your name as your business name instead, since technically the EIN is assigned to your name first and to your business name secondarily.

II

Small Business Administration

6

Banking and Payments

Choosing a Bank Account

When you start a business, one of the best things you can do to make financial management easier is to open a business bank account. Even if you are running a Sole Proprietorship, it's helpful to keep separate accounts. It will make it easier to track earnings and expenses. Luckily, there are plenty of free options available, and many will even help you save for taxes or different goals. Most also give you a debit card.

Two options I like are Found Business Banking and Relay Business Banking. I have an account with each one for two different businesses. Both are free but have paid versions if you need more feature. The free versions already include a debit card, let you create sub-accounts, and allow you to send and create invoices. They each have an app so that you can bank from your phone.

Relay is a bit more like a standard bank account. You'll get a checking and savings account, and you can create additional accounts if you want to allocate money for specific purposes. For example, you could allocate money for taxes or for the purchase of supplies. Relay also helps you track purchases by asking you to email receipts for larger purchases and saving them for you.

Found gives you a checking account only, but allows you to create 'pockets' which are like sub-accounts that you can use to separate your funds. You can also create a pocket for taxes and Found will calculate how much you should put aside. Found will also help you categorize purchases and will track which purchases are business expenses for tax purposes. This is very helpful when you file taxes because you can import all of your transactions into most tax software.

When choosing a bank, you want to consider any recurring fees like monthly account fees. You should also find out if you'll receive a debit card, since debit cards are great for making business purchases directly from your account. In addition, if being able to check on your finances from your phone is important to you, you'll want an option that offers an app.

Being able to create pockets or sub-accounts is very useful and something I look for in a banking service. It makes it easy to separate out funds that are available for purchases, funds that you're saving for taxes, and funds that you want to use for recurring expenses, for example. Invoice creation and automatic tax allocation are two more features to to look for. Some banks, like Relay, offer business accounts and business credit cards, so if that is important to you, look for one that offers both.

In most cases, a bank with physical locations will have more fees than a bank that is solely online. If you are concerned about being able to deposit cash, even online-only banks usually have options that allow this through participating stores. Found allows deposits through stores like Dollar General and 7Eleven using a barcode that you receive in the app. Relay lets you deposit cash through Allpoint ATMs and certain retailers.

Overall, Found is a bit simpler, while Relay is a bit more robust. But both are great options, as are many of the other banking providers out there. As long as you know which features are important to you, you'll be able to find the right option for your business. And remember, you can always switch banks! This is not a decision you need to be stuck with if your current bank isn't right for you.

One more thing you need to know is that some banks will only let LLCs or other registered entities create an account. So if you're a sole proprietor, make sure you choose a bank that will accept you. Good news is, most will.

Accepting Customer Payments

In addition to a business bank account, in most cases you will need a way to easily accept in-person payments from customers. While cash is a great option, not everyone will want to pay with cash. Most customers also expect you to accept Venmo, Cash App, or credit card payments.

Venmo and Cash App are easy to set up and easy to use. Download the app of your choice onto your phone and create a personal account if you don't have one already. Once you have your personal account, you'll be able to go into your account settings and create a business account. In Cash App, just tap on the icon in the top right corner and scroll all the way down. There you will see the option to 'create a business account'. Click and complete the account setup process. In Venmo, tap the 'Me' button in the bottom left corner, then tap the top left corner where it shows your profile name. Click 'Create a business profile' and follow the prompts.

While Cash App and Venmo will charge you a small fee for each payment made to your business account, you are supposed to use a business account for these transactions and not your personal account. That's because Venmo and Cash App personal accounts are only designed to be used for payments from friends and family. So to be in compliance, you should create and use a business account.

To accept Cash App and Venmo payments from your customers, you'll just need to print out your QR code or your account name so that customers can easily pay you. You can do this by taking a screenshot of your QR code, cropping it, and then printing it out. If you're not sure how to find your QR code, select the option for accepting or requesting a payment and there should be a button that will show your QR code. You'll also want to connect your business bank account or debit card to Cash App and Venmo so that you can transfer money out after customers pay you.

To accept credit card payments, you'll need to sign up with a payment processor. Square is one of the easiest and cheapest options. There is no monthly fee but you'll be charged a credit card processing fee as a percentage of each payment. This fee is usually around 3%. Square will also send you a mini card reader that attaches to your phone. This lets you accept payments from credit cards that don't have a chip. For chip cards, you will be able to charge them by touching the card to your phone. It is very convenient and easy to set up.

To get started, you can download the Square app and create an account, or you can make an account at **squareup.com/us/en/hardware/reader** using a computer. Find and click the 'reader for magstripe' option and click on 'get first reader free'. Once you've created your account, you can go into the app settings and start adding your products onto the app. That way when people make a purchase, you can just select the items and add them to the cart. Alternatively, you can skip this step and just manually input the sales total for each sale. Square is relatively intuitive to use, so it's a good starting option.

While there are payment systems that don't charge you a percentage of sales, such as National Bank Card, they will usually charge you a monthly fee instead, or have you buy an expensive card reader. But once you've made some sales, you can look into those options if you like. However, instead charging the credit card processing charge to you, they will add it on to the total and charge the customer. This may or may not be ok with your customers.

While Shopify also offers similar options to Square, I find Square a bit easier to set up and use. But if you have a Shopify website and are selling the same products at the same prices in person, Shopify can be a good option for you. You can just download the Shopify app and they will also send you a small card reader for chip cards. You may not be able to accept magnet stripe cards though. The app is also not quite as intuitive as Square. But if you already have a Shopify website, it makes sense to also use their app to accept payments.

7

Revenue Tracking

When you're running a business, it's important to know how much you're spending and how much you're earning. It's also helpful to track which items you've sold so that you know what is most popular. I find that the easiest way to do this is with a spreadsheet. But if you have a business bank account and all your earnings go into the account while all of your spending comes out of that account, that might be enough for you. You will be able to see your total earnings and spending easily, but you won't know what exactly you sold to earn your income. It also won't be as helpful if you are adding funds to your business account from your personal account or if you are spending funds from other accounts or credit cards.

Spreadsheets are nice because you can track exactly what is important to you. If you need to pay Sales Tax you can even set your spreadsheet up by the Sales Tax calendar instead of by months. That way it will be really easy to see what you earned in each taxable period.

It is also a good idea to track your expenses in detail, so by writing down what exactly you bought. That way you can see if there are items you don't need to buy in the future or if there are expenses that are recurring each month. You will also need to know what types of items you bought for your business when you do your taxes.

Your spreadsheet should also contain formulas that will calculate totals for you. But don't worry, I will give you an example spreadsheet that you can copy and adjust to your needs.

I use Google Sheets for all my spreadsheets because it is easy and also free. With a little practice, you can do a lot with Google Sheets. I've created a tracker that you can copy and then edit.

The link for this spreadsheet is **docs.google.com/spreadsheets/d/103wXVv 2uKgvz9ukUOXsr0tsARERnLrnkK1w6lWXVbJI/edit?usp=sharing.** I've also included a QR code for easier access. You will have view-only access, so you will need to make a copy of the spreadsheet so that you can edit it. Just click on 'file' in the top left and then on 'make a copy'. I've also added a Password tab and a Business Info tab to this spreadsheet to help you keep track of important information.

This tracker will automatically input the date of each entry and will calculate totals for you, both for spending and earning. In the Earned section, you can enter the total you earned on a given day if you sold multiple items and then put the location in the description. Or, you can list each item sold and then write down the item in the description. You can track your sales and spending by month and also specify if the sale included sales tax or not. You do have to select an option or the amount will be left out of the total. But you can use this spreadsheet whether or not your items are taxable.

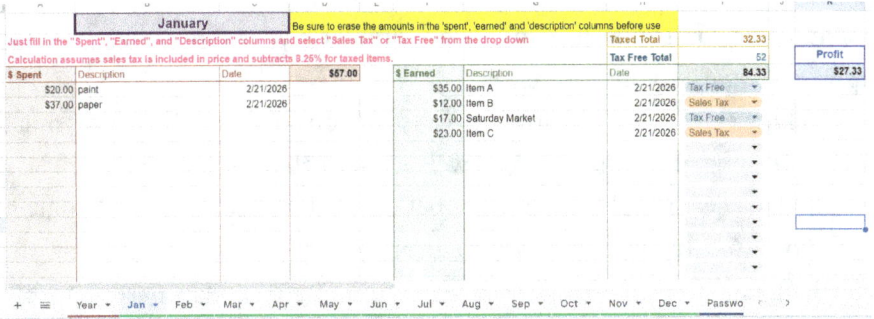

January tab with monthly totals and the ability to specify taxable and non-taxable sales

On the "Year" tab, you can see totals for each month, as well as separate totals for taxable sales and sales tax due dates. I have designed this spreadsheet with the assumption that you are adding sales tax to your prices rather than calculating it at the end of each sale. So when you indicate that a sale was taxable, the spreadsheet will subtract sales tax from the total you enter. This way you know how much to report as your total taxable sales amount when you remit sales tax, and you know what your true profit is because the sales tax you collected has already been subtracted. The profit calculation includes taxable and un-taxed sales, minus any sales tax.

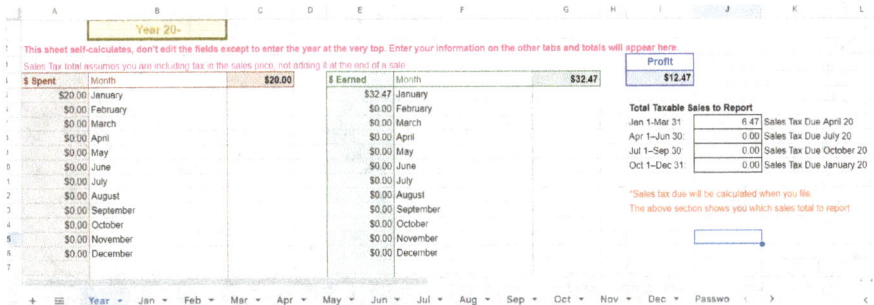

Year tab with totals for the entire year and taxable sales separated out for reporting purposes

If you like, you can of course create your own spreadsheet, or even track sales and spending using a paper notebook. But this will at least give you a starting point. If you don't know how to create a formula in your spreadsheet, you can usually google it to find an answer.

Tracking earnings is important because not only will it tell you how much you are selling, it can also tell how well you are selling at each location. So if you attend several different markets but do much better at one of them, you can choose to attend that one more frequently. Or if you see that your sales are much higher around holidays, you can look for more holiday markets to join.

While you may not make a profit right away, you'll be able to see if you are spending too much or if you can afford to buy some additional items for your business. You can also track how you do over time. A year from today might look very different than the first month of your business. It's a really useful way to see how your business is doing, and also really helpful for tax return time and remitting sales tax.

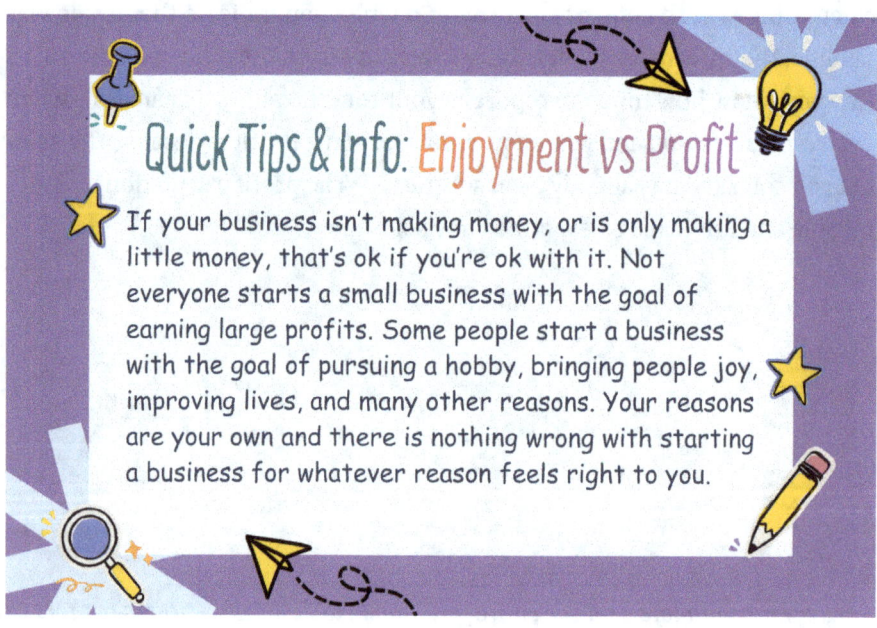

Quick Tips & Info: Enjoyment vs Profit

If your business isn't making money, or is only making a little money, that's ok if you're ok with it. Not everyone starts a small business with the goal of earning large profits. Some people start a business with the goal of pursuing a hobby, bringing people joy, improving lives, and many other reasons. Your reasons are your own and there is nothing wrong with starting a business for whatever reason feels right to you.

8

Sales and Use Tax

Collecting Sales Tax

Most small business owners need to collect sales tax. There are only a few exceptions and these are generally for food items. Items you make or services you sell are taxable.

Non-taxable items are generally foods that are meant for later consumption. For example, vegetables, fruits, bakery items, and canned foods are usually not meant to be eaten immediately. But, if you sell small cakes and you give out a fork with your items, you would need to collect sales tax because that's a sign that the food is meant to be eaten immediately. Food trucks would also need to collect sales tax because they sell ready-to-eat food. However, if you sell a loaf of bread or a cinnamon roll with the intention that someone will eat your product at home (and no utensils are included), you don't need to collect sales tax. Even vegetable seedlings are generally not taxed.

Generally, if you sell items or provide services, other than these food exceptions, you will need to collect sales tax. Sales tax is 8.25% of the sale price in basically all areas. That includes 6.25% of State tax and 2% local tax. Also be aware that you are not allowed to collect sales tax unless you have a sales tax permit, known as a "Sales and Use Tax Permit". So be sure you apply for one before you start selling taxable items. Later, you will have to remit, or pass on, the sales tax you collected to the Texas Comptroller.

You can add sales tax on top of your sales price when people make purchases, or you can include it in the price from the beginning. Generally, it is easier to calculate your prices with sales tax included since it prevents you from having to collect a lot of small change. If you include sales tax in the price, you need to display a sign that says "Texas state and local sales and use tax is included in the sales price". You'll also need to do a small amount of math when you report your sales.

If you are including sales tax in the item's price, you will need to divide your total sales by 1.0825 to get the amount you need to remit sales tax on. So if you collected a total of $530 from sales, but this total includes sales tax, you can't report that you need to remit sales tax for $530. This would imply that $530 is your pre-tax sales total and if you report that as the amount to be taxed, you will overpay. Instead, you need to report that your sales totaled $530 divided by 1.0825, which comes out to $489.60. This calculation will remove the sales tax you collected from your earnings. In this example, you would have collected $40.39 in sales tax, which is the amount you should remit. But if you say that your sales totaled $530 then you will have to pay 8.25% of that to the government, which is $43.72. That's more sales tax than you actually collected, and more than you should remit.

Resale Exception

If you are selling items to another business for resale, you do not need to collect sales tax. Instead, sales tax would be collected when the items are bought by the end customer. But you are required to get a Texas Sales and Use Tax Resale Certificate from the business. This form explains why you didn't collect sales tax and should be kept in your records for 4 years.

Note that this form includes two versions of the certificate. The first version requires the Texas Sales and Use Tax Permit Number of the purchaser but the second version does not. You can have the business complete either version of the form.

How to Apply for a Sales and Use Tax Permit

To apply for a Sales and Use Tax Permit, go to **comptroller.texas.gov/taxe s/permit** and click on 'Apply for Permit via eSystems'. If you don't have an account, you will need to create one. You'll also need to provide information about your business, and you'll need your NAICS code. This code signifies the type of business you are doing. Just do a search using **naics.com/search** and enter a keyword related to the type of business you will be doing. Then, chose the NAICS code that best matches your business and enter it when asked.

Write down the code you've chosen and keep with your records. When you file income taxes you may be asked to provide it. Once you complete the form, your tax permit and a paper tax return will be mailed to you. You will need to display the permit wherever you do business. Make sure you keep the blank tax return in your files! You'll need this when you remit your sales tax.

When you apply for your sales tax permit, the system will also tell you how often you need to pay sales tax. It will likely be quarterly but could be more frequent. You will also receive email reminders before your sales taxes are due.

How to Remit Sales and Use Tax

To remit the sales tax you collected, go to **comptroller.texas.gov/taxes/file-p ay** and select 'Sales and Use Taxes' next to your business' name. If you don't see your business listed, you need to add it. Click on 'Assign Tax/Fees'. On the next page, enter your 11-digit taxpayer number. You can find this number listed on your Texas Sales and Use Tax Permit. It is also on the paper Texas Sales and Use Tax Return that the Comptroller sent you along with your Texas Sales and Use Permit. While you can file the paper version, it is much easier to file online.

Once you've entered your taxpayer number, press 'continue'. On the right side near the bottom, click on 'Assign', then enter your WebFile number. You can find the WebFile number at the very top edge of the paper tax return that the Comptroller sent you. It starts with "RT" followed by several numbers.

Then click 'Assign' and 'Submit Changes'. On the next page, agree to the disclaimer and click 'Continue'.

Now, under 'My Taxpayer Accounts' you will see your name listed (if it's a Sole Proprietorship) or your business name listed (for LLCs), and next to that it will say 'Sales and Use Tax'. Click on 'Sales and Use Tax' and select 'File Original Return'. Select the current period, click 'Continue', then 'Continue' on the next page. You will be asked if you are taking credits. You can find more details here **comptroller.texas.gov/help/sales-tax/credits-exports.php**. But basically, you can say you are taking credits if you paid sales tax in error on items that you purchased for your business but that should have been tax-exempt, or if you paid sales tax to the Comptroller on items that were returned by your customer. Make your selection and continue on to the next question.

You will get to a page titled 'Original Return for Period Ending'. If you had no sales at all, you can check the box at the top that says 'check this box and click continue if all amounts are zero'. Otherwise, you will need to enter the taxable amount of your business' sales made in Texas for the period listed in the box that says 'Total Texas Sales'. This includes ALL of your Texas sales, whether they were taxable or not. In the 'Taxable Sales' box, enter the amount of taxable sales made in Texas. Make sure you don't include the amount you collected for sales tax (see the previous section for help calculating this). Note that if you only sell taxable items, your amounts for 'Total Texas Sales' and 'Taxable Sales' will be the same.

In the final box, enter the amount of all purchases, whether personal or for your business, that are taxable but that you did not pay taxes on. Include purchases made in all states. Exclude items purchased solely for resale. It is highly likely that this will be zero, unless you mistakenly bought items using a tax exempt status and then later realized you were supposed to pay taxes on them. If you had no purchases that you still need to pay sales tax on, enter "0". Press 'Continue'.

If you had taxable sales, you will need to enter which amount of sales occurred in which jurisdiction. For example, if you sell at farmer's markets in two different counties, you need to enter how much you sold at each location. Enter the amount, and press "Continue". On the next page, you will be shown how much state tax you need to remit and how much local tax you need to remit. Click 'Continue' if everything looks right. If not, edit the information.

On the next page, you can pay with a credit card, electronic check, or submit your return without paying. If you want to pay later, you can log back into your account, but instead of selecting 'File Original Return', you would select the option to 'Make a Payment Only'. Proceed through the payment screens to submit payment using your chosen method. When you're done, print out the confirmation page or save it to your computer. Keep it with your other business records.

How to Cancel a Sales and Use Tax Permit

Fill out the form at **comptroller.texas.gov/web-forms/manage-account/c lose-location.** However this form also closes at least one of your business locations. If you only have one location then it closes that location. But, if you are no longer collecting sales and use tax then it is probably because you are closing your business.

9

Liability Insurance

L iability insurance is an option for both Sole Proprietorships and LLCs. It protects your business in the case of accidental injury or damages. It also protects you if you are accused of making a mistake, whether or not you actually did. It can cover spaces you rent as well as damage or injury that occurs when doing business in your own home. In some cases, farmers or craft markets will require proof of liability insurance before letting you join. Liability insurance can also give you peace of mind on top of the actual protection that it offers.

Food Businesses

If you sell food, you should consider purchasing food liability insurance. This insurance will protect you if someone gets sick after eating something you sold. It will often cover general liability claims as well, such as damage or injury to people and property other than that of yourself and your employees. Most policies start at around $25 per month. One of the best options for liability insurance for food businesses is **fliprogram.com**. Their policies are specifically designed for food businesses and also cover sales at markets and general liability. You'll find that most other insurance companies don't cover small businesses that sell food.

Craft Businesses

Craft businesses may be less likely to need liability insurance, but it is still a good idea and gives you peace of mind. And if you sell at markets, some of them will require it. That way if one of your products accidentally injures someone, or a customer trips at your booth, you will be protected. You can even add theft coverage in case someone steals from your booth. It will usually start at about $25 per month. For farmers markets, **actinsurance.com/farme rs-markets-insurance** is a good option to look into.

If you sell online only, or online and in person, they have coverage for that as well. Go to **actinsurance.com/online-retailer-insurance** and read through their offers. This coverage also starts at $25 per month, but you can also choose the per-event option if that suits you better. Just be aware that this insurance does not cover food sales, only craft sales.

Service Businesses

If you provide a service, such as massage, hair care, pet care, etc, you will want liability insurance that covers any injury or damage to your customers or their property. Some customers will only hire you if you are insured, and for your own protection, insurance is a smart option. You can get a quote at **acuity.com/business/service-business-insurance**. You can also check out **hiscox.com/sb-lp/general-liability** for small-business options.

Do I Really Need Insurance?

You might be wondering if you really need insurance when you are just starting out. Maybe you've barely made any sales or you just don't think your business is particularly risky. I am not a lawyer or an insurance expert. So while insurance will definitely offer you protection, I don't know if you will need it. Maybe no one will ever have any issues with your business, but maybe they will. There really is no way to know. But the less you sell and the fewer people you interact with, the lower your exposure to risk should hypothetically be.

However, for the best advice, I recommend speaking with a lawyer who has experience with small business liability. As a disclaimer, I am not liable for any choices you do or do not make based on what I have written here.

10

File Your Tax Return

Tax Filing Methods

When it comes to filing your income tax return, you have several options. You can file manually by printing out the paper forms from the IRS website and mailing them. You can use a tax filing software to help you fill out the correct forms and submit them. Or you can hire a tax preparation specialist to file for you using the documents you provide them.

My preferred method is to use a filing software. I feel like it is a good balance between doing it myself but also having some help. I trust that I won't be missing any forms or inputting information in the wrong sections. Good filing options are Turbo Tax, Tax Act, and Free Tax USA. As the name says, Free Tax USA is completely free even for businesses.

I don't really recommend printing and filling out the forms manually since they look much more confusing printed out as compared to answering relevant questions using tax software. Also, it is up to you to figure out which forms you need to fill out and how to do so. But if you have a very simple tax return, you really like working with pen and paper, or you have a lot of experience with filing taxes, you may prefer this method. However, a major downside is that if you don't fill out all the correct forms then there is no one (except the

IRS) to tell you that you missed something.

If you prefer that a professional does your taxes, you can contact a local H&R Block office or search for a CPA (Certified Public Accountant) or tax preparer online and then choose one you like. But this is probably going to be more expensive than using a tax software. And unless your taxes are really complicated you can likely do it yourself. I do recommend contacting a tax professional if you are running a multi-member LLC or a partnership. When there is more than one business owner, things get complicated quickly and special forms are required.

In this chapter, I do my best to explain how to file taxes for your business. But please be aware that I am not a tax preparer, CPA, or accounting professional. While this information is as accurate as I could make it, there may still be inaccuracies. This chapter is not to be taken as tax advice, but rather as general information. For help with your specific situation, it is best to contact a tax professional.

Sole Proprietorships and Single Member LLCs

Filing your income tax return when you own a Sole Proprietorship or an LLC is not that different from regular filing. It all goes on the same return and is due by April 15th. Your business income gets combined with all of your other income. The process is the same for an LLC as for a Sole Proprietorship as long as you are the only business owner. If you are married and your spouse is also an owner, the process is still the same except that in some sections you will enter information for each person separately by dividing earnings and expenses between the two of you.

I usually file with Turbo Tax, but this year, since I am writing this book, I decided to also try Free Tax USA so that I could tell you about it. I found that while Turbo Tax is nice because it has my previous information stored, switching to Free Tax USA was not difficult. I was able to import last year's tax return, and most of my basic information was transferred over. Completing the return was also quite simple, and one nice difference was that I didn't have a lot of issues to fix at the end. Turbo Tax tends to ask me to fill in specific fields on certain forms that it missed initially, and it can be hard to understand what is needed. So if you are looking for a free tax filing software, Free Tax USA is a good option and doesn't charge extra for business filings.

If you want to be sure you're using the best option, you can also complete the process on more than one website and see which gives you the best result. Then again, I may be the only person to ever do that. But when using a paid software, you do only get charged at the very end when you submit your return.

If you file using a tax software, you might be asked a few questions before you begin. Questions such as, did you buy a house, did you withdraw from a retirement account, did you start a business, and more. You should answer these accurately so that the right forms will be assigned to you. If you're using Turbo Tax you'll likely be shown a tax filing option that includes Expert Assist. This is a real person that you can ask for help with your taxes, but it does cost more. If you don't want this option, just click below where it says 'See other Turbo Tax products'. Choose your best fit. I find that the 'Do it yourself' option still provides plenty of help and explanation while filing your taxes.

If you are using a different tax software, it will look a bit different but overall should be similar. Free Tax USA will jump right in without asking a lot of questions, but it lays out all your options as you work through your return.

If you want to file by mail and do the entire process manually, you will need to fill out form 1040 and Schedule C. You can find form 1040 at this link **irs.gov/forms-pubs/about-form-1040** and Schedule C at this link **irs.gov/forms-pubs/about-schedule-c-form-1040**. If your profits were more than $400 you also need to file Schedule SE, found at **irs.gov/taxtopics/tc554.** Then you'll need to mail it to the address listed here for Texas **irs.gov/filing/where-to-file-paper-tax-returns-with-or-without-a-payment**.

Schedule C

The main difference when filing for a business as compared to a standard tax return is that you'll file Schedule C along with the usual form 1040. If you and your spouse are in business together, you will need to split expenses and proceeds in half and assign them to each of you, even if you are married filing jointly. Luckily this isn't hard to do and your software should walk you through it.

When filing taxes for your business, you'll need to know when you started your business and how much you earned and spent. You should also have your EIN ready if you have one. If you paid an individual contractor more than $600, you will need to send them form 1099-NEC. If you file with Turbo Tax, they will help you fill this out. You can also find this form online and complete it. If you paid a business for services and not an individual person, you don't need to send them a 1099-NEC. It only applied to individuals.

You'll be asked if you use the cash accounting method or the accrual method. The cash accounting method mean you count your income in the year you receive it, so it is the most common. You'll also be asked if you received form 1099. 1099-NEC is for payment to someone who did work but is not an employee. So if you did work for someone as a contractor you might receive this form.

1099-K is for payments that went through an electronic payment platform. So if you were paid through Venmo, Cash App, PayPal, Square, etc and it was for more than 200 transactions or for more than $20,000 total, you may receive a 1099-K. If you were paid less than that, you won't receive a form but you still have to report the income.

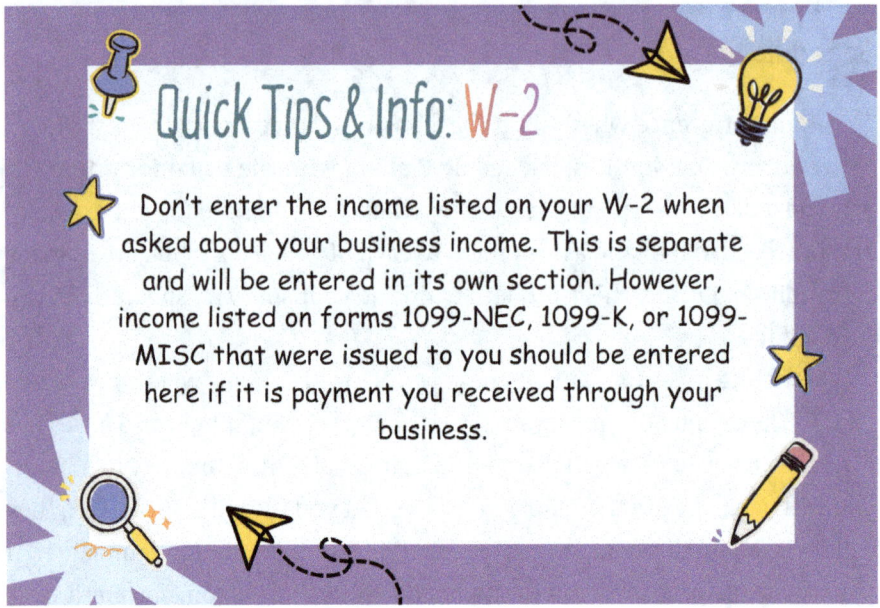

Quick Tips & Info: W-2

Don't enter the income listed on your W-2 when asked about your business income. This is separate and will be entered in its own section. However, income listed on forms 1099-NEC, 1099-K, or 1099-MISC that were issued to you should be entered here if it is payment you received through your business.

You'll be asked about your expenses as well. If you used a dedicated business account and are using Turbo Tax, you will likely be able to log in and import all of your transactions. This will make everything much easier. But if not, it's enough if you've tracked your expenses in a spreadsheet. You'll be asked to enter the amounts you spent in each category.

Some filing software may ask you whether your investment is at risk or not. This is for a check box on Schedule C to determines whether you used your own money to set up your business. If you did, you will answer that "All investment is at risk". For most entrepreneurs, the answer will be yes, because you've most likely put your own money into your business. An exception would be a loan that you aren't required to pay back, and a few other instances where investments are guaranteed against loss, which is not common. Turbo Tax may ask you this but Free Tax USA seems to answer this based on your other responses. Unfortunately every tax software is a little different.

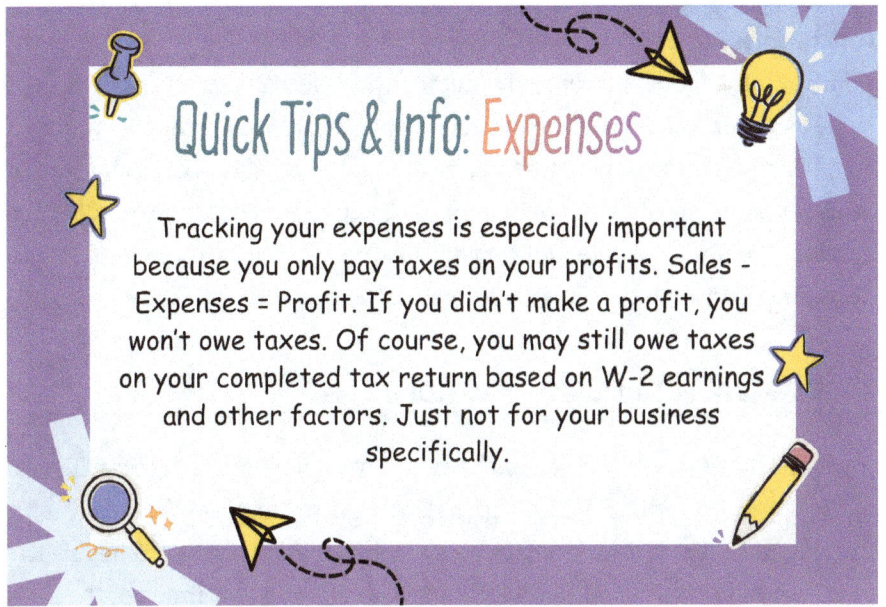

Quick Tips & Info: Expenses

Tracking your expenses is especially important because you only pay taxes on your profits. Sales - Expenses = Profit. If you didn't make a profit, you won't owe taxes. Of course, you may still owe taxes on your completed tax return based on W-2 earnings and other factors. Just not for your business specifically.

Schedule SE

If your profits for the year were $400 or more, you will need to complete Schedule SE. Your tax software will lead you through this or use the information you've already provided to complete the form for you. Schedule SE calculates the amount of Self-Employment taxes you owe. This tax applies to 92.35% of your profits, so a small percentage of your profits will not be subject to this tax. But the rest of your profits will be taxed 12.4% for Social Security and 2.9% for Medicare. There is an additional 0.9% Medicate tax if you earned more than a certain amount, as of this writing, that is more than $200,000 if filing as single, or more than $250,000 if married and filing jointly. But you can deduct half of your self employment taxes as a business expense, which will help reduce the amount. Your tax filing software or preparer will likely do this for you automatically.

You'll of course need to complete the rest of your tax return as well, likely by entering information from your W-2 if you work for an employer, and any other sections that apply to you. But there is nothing else you need to do for your business taxes.

I also want to quickly remind you that your income tax return is not the same as remitting sales tax. Your income tax return tells you how much, if any, taxes you owe on money you earned. Remitting sales tax is the return of sales tax that you collected on behalf of the government and is filed on the Secretary of State website, not on your tax return. You can see chapter 8 on Sales and Use Tax for a refresher if this applies to you.

Multi-Member LLCs or Partnerships

If your business has more than one owner or member, your business will need to file Form 1065 with the IRS, and it also needs to create a Schedule K-1 for each member. Then, each member uses the information on their Schedule K-1 to fill out their own Schedule C. Schedule K-1 tells you how much of the LLCs earnings and losses apply to you, so that you can pay taxes on your portion of profits if there are any.

Form 1065 is an informational form that the IRS requires. It can be filed using Turbo Tax Business, TaxAct, FreeTaxUSA and similar software. Only one member of the business needs to file this. Schedule K-1 can also be created using filing software. However, taxes for a multi-member LLC or partnership get a bit more complicated so I would recommend that you consult a CPA or tax professional for the most accurate filing. Also note that both Form 1065 and Schedule K-1 are due by March 15th, not the standard April 15th deadline.

Quick Tips & Info: Married Couples

A 2-person LLC where the members are married will file taxes as if it were a single-member LLC. When you file as "Married filing jointly" you will be able to file for both members using only Schedule C and Schedule SE (depending on total profits of course).

LLC Filing as an S Corp

If your business is earning significant profits, filing as an S Corporation can be beneficial by reducing your medicare and social security taxes. To file as an S Corp, you need to fill out form 2553. You can do this even after your LLC is already formed, since this is just a tax election.

S Corps require you to run payroll because you will now be treated as an employee of the LLC instead of as an owner. You can then receive a salary which will have employment taxes taken out of it, but you can also receive part of your profits as a distribution payment, which will not have employment taxes taken out.

Because of this, in some cases it can reduce your medicare and social security taxes. But it is a more complicated filing and is best completed with the help of an accountant who can also help you determine if this filing method is right for you. You can read more here **nolo.com/legal-encyclopedia/electing-s-c orporation-tax-status-single-member-llc.html**. Most recommendations state that your profits should be at least $40,000 to benefit from an S Corp selection. But businesses earning a profit of $60,000 or more see the most benefits.

If you want a system that helps you manage payroll, taxes, and other S Corp subjects, check out **collective.com** or similar options. They can take over some of the additional administrative and tax related tasks required when running your business as an S Corp.

Do You Need to Pay Quarterly Taxes?

You might have heard of quarterly taxes and you may be wondering if this applies to you. Normally, you'll know if you need to pay quarterly taxes because the IRS will tell you to. The idea behind quarterly taxes is to have you pay taxes regularly throughout the year instead of paying all at once when you file your tax return. Quarterly taxes can be required whether or not you own a business. If you owe more than $1,000 when you file your taxes, you are supposed to pay quarterly estimated taxes every 3 months.

The IRS expects you to pay the amount you owed the previous year, divided into 4 payments. To be extra safe, you can pay 110% of what you owed the previous year. That's the amount required for those filing jointly who earned more than $150,000 or who are filing separately and earned more than $75,000. You can face a penalty if you don't do this. You can pay online using one of the methods listed here **irs.gov/payments**. You can even pay on the IRS app **irs.gov/help/irs2goapp**.

Most people pay their taxes throughout the year because they are automatically taken out of your paycheck based on you W-4 form. That's the form your job has you fill out when you get hired to tell them how much to take out for taxes. But this only applies to W-2 jobs, which are jobs that send you a W-2 at the end of the year which tells you how much you earned and how much taxes were taken out. Contractors and businesses don't have taxes paid out of their paychecks. That's why they are more likely to be required to pay quarterly taxes.

Alternatively, you can set aside 20% to 30% of your profits as you get paid and then submit that amount as your quarterly tax payment. This is where a business bank account such with sub-accounts, like Relay or Found, is helpful. You'll be able to set aside a percentage automatically. Some accounts will also let you create a sub-account specifically for taxes and will estimate the amount you'll owe and save it for you. Then you can pay the amount you've put aside by the quarterly tax due date. It is relatively simple to do online and you won't have to edit your W-4 to do it. Of course, if you don't have a W-2 job then you'll likely be required to pay quarterly taxes since you won't have another way of regularly paying them.

Quarterly tax periods and due dates:

Jan. 1–March 31 due April 15

April 1–May 31 due June 15

June 1–Aug. 31 sue Sept. 15

Sept. 1–Dec. 31 Jan. 15* of the following year.

What if you don't want to pay quarterly taxes and you have a W-2 job? Good news! You can submit a new W-4 form to have an additional amount of taxes taken out instead of paying quarterly. You can talk to your HR department or look at your payroll account to find this form. If you are married and don't work a W-2 job, but your spouse does and you file as married filing jointly, your spouse can edit their W-4 instead to take out additional taxes.

There are a few ways to figure out how much you should pay in additional taxes. If you owed more than $1,000 last year, you can divide the amount you owed by 52 if you get paid weekly, or by 26 if you get paid bi-weekly. Then add that amount on your W-4 where it says "Extra withholding. Enter any additional tax you want withheld each pay period". This should be near the bottom, line 4(c).

Another way to calculate is by entering 25% or 30% of your expected business profit as the extra withholding amount on line 4(c). This should get you very close to the amount you'll owe. Some businesses put aside just 20% for taxes, so there is a bit of a range. 30% is safest, but a smaller percentage will still help you when you file your taxes. As long as the total amount you owe when you complete your tax return is less than $1,000, you won't have to pay quarterly taxes.

You can also sign up for a management site that helps you figure out your quarterly taxes and helps you with filing. You can look into **gusto.com/go/pro duct/price** and **collective.com** for their options, or find a similar service. They do charge for their services but can be helpful especially if you have employees or an S Corp.

Now you know how to file taxes for you business! While it may seem complicated, it is very doable with a tax filing software, especially if you file as a single member LLC or a sole proprietor. When in doubt, most filing software will give you the option to ask a real person for help. And of course you can always go to a tax specialist or accountant for more complicated cases. I do recommend you go to a professional if you are not the only owner of your business, since filing taxes will be more complicated. And as a disclaimer, I am not a tax professional and this information is not to be taken as tax advice, it is general information only.

11

Business Records

E asy access to important business documents makes running a small business much easier and less chaotic. This is a list of documents that I recommend you keep so that you can find them easily. A binder or file folder works well for paper copies, but you should create a folder on your computer as well. That way you can easily email or upload documents when you apply for bank accounts or join farmers markets.

Keep Paper Copies Of:

- Sales and Use Tax documents
- EIN
- LLC Operating Agreement (if applicable)
- LLC Certificate of Formation
- LLC Certificate of Filing
- Sales Tax payment receipts (if applicable)
- Print outs of any online filings you've made
- Assumed Name Certificate
- Personal Tax Returns

Keep Electronic Copies Of:

- EIN
- LLC Operating Agreement (if applicable)
- LLC Certificate of Formation
- LLC Certificate of Filing
- Personal Tax Returns
- Any other documents that you are asked to submit electronically
- NAICS code (write down for future reference)
- Sales Tax remission receipts
- Photos of your products
- Photos of your market set-up, if applicable
- Notes on sales channels that have and have not worked for you

12

Save for Retirement

I f self-employment is your main source of income, you might be wondering about your options for retirement savings. You have several options. You can open a a standard IRA, which is available to anyone who earns an income. You can choose a Solo 401(k), which is only available to business owners. You can create a SEP IRA,which is a retirement account for owners and employees of small businesses. Or you can open a SIMPLE IRA which is another type of retirement account for owners and employees. IRA's are the easiest to set up, while the rest are more complicated and may require specific paperwork and have more rules. I have summarized your options below, in order of simplest to more complicated.

Roth vs Traditional

Before you read about the different retirement accounts, it helps to understand the difference between Roth contributions and Traditional contributions. Roth contributions come from income you've already paid taxes on, so these are after-tax contributions. Because you have already paid income taxes on the amount you're contributing, you don't pay taxes when you withdraw the money at retirement. But you do pay taxes on the contribution amount as part of your income taxes for the year.

Traditional contributions come from pre-tax income, so you don't pay income taxes on the amount you contribute. Instead, the amount you contribute to a Traditional account gets subtracted from your annual income so that you don't pay taxes on it. But, you pay income taxes on your Traditional account when you withdraw the money. At that point, the amount you withdraw will be counted as part of your yearly income and taxed accordingly.

Your tax bracket may change in between the time you contribute and the time you make your withdrawals. So if your tax bracket will be lower when you retire and start making withdrawals, a Traditional IRA may be better for you. If you think your tax bracket is lower today, a Roth IRA may be the better option. Generally, experts expect tax brackets to be higher in the future, meaning that if you qualify, a Roth account is a good option for most people. But if you qualify for both and are unsure which to choose, it is often possible to contribute to both options.

Some Roth accounts also have income limits, so if you earn more than a certain amount, you can't contribute to a Roth account. Usually your account will ask you this to help you contribute correctly.

Roth: Contributions come from income you already paid taxes on. Withdrawals are not taxed.

Traditional: Contributions are subtracted from your income and not taxed. Withdrawals are taxed.

IRA (Individual Retirement Account)

An IRA is the simplest way to save for retirement since you can set it up for yourself just by creating an account with brokerage firm or financial institution of your choice. Anyone who has earned income can contribute to an IRA, whether self-employed or not. You can choose between a Roth IRA and a Traditional IRA.

Roth IRAs have an income limit, which means that if you earn more than the limit you cannot open a Roth IRA but you can open a Traditional IRA. For 2026, people filing as single are ineligible for a Roth IRA if they earn more than $168,000 and married people if they earn more than $252,000.

The amount you can contribute annually adjusts each year, so it is best to confirm the maximum at the start of each new year. For 2026, you can contribute $7,500 to your IRA, and an extra $1,100 catch-up contribution per year if you are 50 and over.

As is the case with retirement accounts, there is a penalty for early IRA withdrawals. You must wait until you reach retirement age of $59^{1/2}$ to withdraw penalty-free. You also must taking distributions from your IRA by age 72 at the latest.

- *Roth (after-tax contributions) or Traditional (pre-tax contributions)*
- *Withdraw at 59 1/2*
- *Max contribution $7,500*
- *Catch up contribution for 50 and over $1,100*
- *Anyone with income can open an IRA*
- *For businesses with or without employees, but does not include employees*

Solo 401(k)

A Solo 401(k) is an option you can choose if your business has no employees or if you and your spouse are the only employees. If you have any full-time employees you can't use this plan. That's why it's called a "solo" plan - it's just for you. You also need an EIN to sign up for this plan.

The Solo 401(k) plan allows you to contribute once as your employer and once as an employee. And yes, both the employer and the employee are you. As the employee, you can contribute up to 100% of your pay or up to $24,500 total, whichever is less. If you are over 50 you can contribute an extra $8,000 and if you are 60-63 an extra $11,250 as a catch-up contribution.

As the employer, you can contribute an additional 25% of your compensation, which will actually come out to be 20% of your net business earnings due to some complicated math. Feel free to read about it here if you're interested **obliviousinvestor.com/digging-into-solo-401k-contribution-limit-math**. You can use the handy calculator here to tell you exactly how much you can contribute as the employee and employer based on your annual profits **obliviousinvestor.com/solo-401k-contribution-calculator**. The maximum contribution, combining both employee and employer, is $72,000 for 2026. But be sure to check the limits each year.

This account is relatively simple to set up through your chosen brokerage. You can add your spouse as well, and they will also be able to contribute up to $72,000 per year. You also don't need to contribute every year. Note that if you also have other 401(k)s, such as through an employer, this limit applies to all 401(k)s belonging to one person, not per 401(k).

If your Solo 401(k) account reaches a balance of more than $250,000, you will need to file form 5500-EZ with the IRS each year. As with other retirement accounts, you can choose to open a Roth account to contribute after-tax dollars, or a Traditional account to contribute pre-tax dollars. And as with other retirement accounts, you'll need to wait until you are 59 1/2 years old before you can make withdrawals.

- *Roth (after-tax contributions) or Traditional (pre-tax contributions)*
- *Withdraw at 59 1/2*
- *Max contribution employer and employee combined $72,000*
- *Employee (that's you) contribution 100% of your pay or up to $24,500 total*
- *Employer (this is also you) contribution up to 20% of net business earnings*
- *Catch up contribution for 50 and over is $8,000, for 60-63 $11,250*
- *File form 5500-EZ with IRS each year the account holds over $250,000*
- *Covers business owner and spouse only, cannot open if you have employees*

SEP IRA (Simplified Employee Pension)

A SEP IRA is for you and your employees if you have any. But you can set this up even if you have no employees. This plan is unique because it is funded only by employer contributions. So as the employer, you will be contributing to everyone's accounts.

To set up a SEP IRA, you need to fill out a form with your plan provider detailing the rules of the plan. This should be a part of the set-up process automatically. Alternatively, you can fill out IRS Form 5305-SEP to record the plan rules and keep it with your business records. You don't send this form to the IRS but you use it to document the rules of your SEP IRA.

You will need to send form 5305-SEP or whichever form or document you used to document the rules of your SEP IRA to all of your employees. The eligibility requirements that you determine apply to both you and to your employees. For example, you can require that employees be at least 18 years old and have worked for you for at least 18 months. The strictest requirement you are allowed to use is that any employee who has worked for you in 3 of the last 5 years for any amount of time is eligible.

You must open a SEP IRA for every eligible employee, or have them open one. You don't have to contribute to the plan every year, but you do have to contribute to every employee's account at an equal percentage during the years that you make contributions. Contributions can be up to 25% of each employees wages. But remember, this doesn't come out of their wages, this is just how you calculate the amount.

For the business owner, the calculation is more complicated since you need to subtract some items, such as half of your self-employment tax, from your profit to determine your net business earnings. You can contribute up to 20% of your net business earnings to your own SEP IRA account. This calculator **obliviousinvestor.com/sep-ira-calculator** will determine your maximum contribution amount for you. For 2026, you cannot contribute more than $72,000 to each account, including your own. Catch-up contributions don't apply to this retirement plan.

You will also need to file Form 5498 with the IRS each year to report the contributions you made. SEP IRAs are usually Traditional accounts, meaning they are funded using pre-tax dollars and the employer can subtract the contributions from their taxable income. But due to new rules, Roth accounts are now also an option. In that case, the employer includes the contribution amount in their taxable income and pays taxes on it. As is standard, withdrawals are allowed after reaching age 59 1/2.

As you can see, a SEP IRA plan is good if you want to contribute to both your own and your employees' retirement funds using your business' profits. But if you don't have employees, the Solo 401(k) does pretty much the same thing and is easier to set up.

- *Roth (after-tax contributions) or Traditional (pre-tax contributions)*
- *Withdraw at 59 1/2*
- *Must create a plan document*
- *Can contribute up to 25% of employee wages to their accounts*
- *Can contribute up to 20% of net business earnings to your own account*
- *All accounts are employer-funded only (employees cannot contribute)*
- *Must contribute equally to all accounts*
- *Must create accounts for all eligible employees*
- *Can contribute some years and not others*
- *Max contribution $72,000 to each account*
- *Must file Form 5498 with the IRS each year to report contributions*
- *For businesses with 0 up to an unspecified number of employees*

SIMPLE IRA (Savings Incentive Match Plan for Employees)

SIMPLE IRA plans accept both employee and employer contributions. They can be established for businesses with a maximum of 100 employees. You can also use this plan if you have no employees. This plan is set up more like a traditional 401(k) in that most of the contribution comes out of the employees' wages while a small percentage comes from the the business (so in this case, from you).

To set up a SIMPLE IRA plan you must fill out IRS form 5304-SIMPLE if employees can choose their own financial institution or 5305-SIMPLE if all employees must have their account held at the financial institution you choose. You can also create your own plan document to establish the accounts, or use one provided by the financial institution you chose to set up your plan. Then keep this document in your business records. You must also give your employees this plan information. You don't need to file anything with the IRS for this plan.

Unlike a SEP IRA, the employer does have to contribute every single year. In fact, the employer is required to match employee contributions up to 3% of their wages, or must contribute 2% to all plan participants even if they are not contributing to their own account.

Employees can choose to contribute up to $17,000 of their salary for 2026 but they are not required to contribute. If the business has 25 or fewer employees, the employee contribution limit increases to $18,100.

As is standard, withdrawals are allowed at 59 1/2 years old. In addition, catch-up contributions of $4,000 are allowed for those 50 or older, and $5,250 for those 60-63. Due to new laws, a SIMPLE IRA can now be either Roth or Traditional, whereas previously they were Traditional only, meaning contributions were always pre-tax.

- Roth (after-tax contributions) or Traditional (pre-tax contributions)
- Withdraw at 59 1/2
- Must create a plan document
- Employee contribution up to $17,000, or up to $18,100 if the business has 25 or fewer employees
- Employer must match employee contributions up to 3% of their wages
- OR employer must contribute 2% of each employee's wages to each account
- Employer must contribute every year
- Employees can contribute if they choose to
- Catch up contribution for 50 and over is $4,000, for 60-63 $5,250
- For businesses with 0 to 100 employees

Account	Who is it for?	Plan Document Required	IRS Filing Requirement	Max Contribution per Account	Employer Contribution	Employee Contribution	Must Employer Contribute Every Year?	Anything Else?
IRA	Any individual who earns an income	No	no	$7,500	None	Up to $7,500	N/A	Easiest set up, not specific to businesses
Solo 401(k)	Business owner and their spouse. CANNOT have employees	No	Yes. Form 5500-EZ if balance greater than $250,000	$72,000	Up to 20% of net business earnings	Up to 100% of your pay or up to $24,500 total, whichever is less	No	You contribute as both the Employer and the Employee
SEP IRA	Businesses with 0 or more employees	Yes	Yes, report contributions on Form 5498 annually	$72,000	Up to 20% of your net business earnings, or 25% of employees' wages	None	No	Employer must contribute to all accounts equally. All eligible employees must have an account
SIMPLE IRA	Businesses with 0 to 100 employees	Yes	no	$17,000 + 3% of wages	3% match, or 2% to all	Up to $17,000	Yes	Employer must match 3% of wages or contribute 2% to all

Comparison of Retirement Accounts for Small Business Owners

Be sure to confirm the contribution limits each year as they update regularly. And of course see a financial advisor for help with your specific situation. This is general information and not meant to be taken as tax or financial advice.

III

Selling Your Products or Services

13

Farm and Craft Markets

I f you want to sell your products in person, one of the easiest ways to get customers is to sell at a location they already know about. I'm talking about farmers and crafters markets. Most cities have at least one farmers market, and they usually accept both food producers and artisans. Some are free to join, but most charge a per-market fee and an annual fee. However, often the fee is affordable. You just need to look around a bit until you find the best market for you and your product. Once you've joined a market, you can also ask other vendors about markets they recommend.

You can start by searching online for farmers markets in your city and cities nearby. You can also search on Facebook and Instagram since most markets are on social media. Then read through their website or social media pages and look for their application and rules. See what the fees are and how often the market sets up. Pick your favorites and go visit in person. Find out if other vendors are selling similar items to what you would be selling, or if your product would make a good addition. See how many customers show up. Talk to a few vendors about their experiences at the market. Talk to the market organizer if possible and find out if they are accepting vendors in your product category and ask any questions you might have.

Some farmers markets are weekly and some are bi-weekly or twice a month. Others are once a month. Some are seasonal while some are year-round. Consider if your product can be sold year-round or not. For example, some candle makers take a break in the summer because their product melts. Many markets slow down in winter as far as customer and vendor participation, even if they meet year-round. If your product can be sold year-round then you might want a year-round market. Or, you can attend multiple markets so that you can sell all year.

Some markets require that you set up each time, while others let you sign up as you are able. Some markets only allow you to miss up to a certain number of market days. There are also seasonal craft market, such as Christmas fairs that are geared towards artisans rather than farmers. Consider who your ideal customer is and where they would shop. There are markets that are better for crafters and others are better for farmers and food producers.

You'll also need to consider the driving distance and cost of each market. If a market is expensive but you do really well, it may be a better option than a market that's free to attend but has few customers. Take the drive into account as well. You may be driving there every weekend, so if you don't like long drives or getting up early, pick a market that's close enough for you to easily get to.

Remember that not all markets are on the weekends. While most markets are on Saturdays, there are also Sunday markets and weekday markets. So even if certain days don't work for you, there is probably a nearby market on a day that you can attend. I suggest visiting different markets and joining your favorites. You are allowed to leave a market and join a different one if it isn't working out.

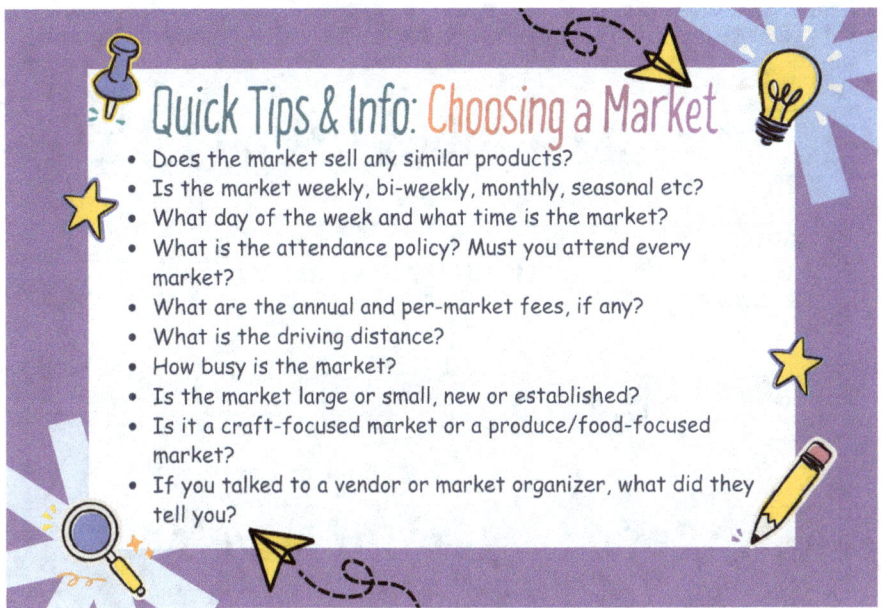

Quick Tips & Info: Choosing a Market
- Does the market sell any similar products?
- Is the market weekly, bi-weekly, monthly, seasonal etc?
- What day of the week and what time is the market?
- What is the attendance policy? Must you attend every market?
- What are the annual and per-market fees, if any?
- What is the driving distance?
- How busy is the market?
- Is the market large or small, new or established?
- Is it a craft-focused market or a produce/food-focused market?
- If you talked to a vendor or market organizer, what did they tell you?

Before your first market, there are items that you will need to buy or borrow. A table and chair are some of the most important. Markets usually require that you have a tablecloth as well, since it looks much nicer. Most vendors also bring a pop-up canopy to protect from the sun and rain and to attach signs to. But for your first few markets you can also show up without one. When you do buy a canopy, you will also need weights to weigh down the legs and keep it from blowing away. This is very important because it is a real issue. Weights are also a required item listed in most market rules for anyone with a canopy. You can buy canopy weights on Amazon or make your own. But just be sure that your weights meet the requirements of the market you are attending. For example, cinder blocks are often not allowed.

Basic Market Supplies

- [ ] Folding table, usually 6ft
- [ ] Chair for you
- [ ] Tablecloth
- [ ] Canopy/pop-up & weights
- [ ] cash bag or box
- [ ] Sales and Use Tax Permit (if applicable)

Once you have your basic supplies, there are a few other things you may need. If you are collecting Sales Tax, you should keep your tax permit in a zip loc bag or other safe protective cover and display it at your table. Most vendors also print or write out pricing signs for their products. And a sign with your business name on it is nice to have as well. I recommend Banner Buzz for custom signs. However, you don't need to have a sign if you don't want to spend the money. But business cards or flyers are a good idea. People will want to know how to find you and how to learn more about your business and products. At my husband's first market, he did not have business cards and he was constantly being asked about them. If you want to give your customers more detailed information about your business or your products, flyers can be helpful. You can design them using Canva or a similar website and then print them out. I like the triple-folded flyers for my business.

A fun way to make pricing signs is to use miniature chalk boards. You can write on them with chalk markers, and they are easy to find on Amazon. And you can wipe them off with a wet cloth and write something new on them if needed. A large A-frame sidewalk chalkboard is an option as well and can help customers see your booth since it makes you stand out. They are also fun to decorate if you are artistically inclined. But again, all you really need for your very first market is a table (preferably folding), a table cloth, and a chair.

If you are accepting cash you should also bring a bag or container with change in it. And if you are accepting Cash App or Venmo, you will want to print out your QR code to make it easier to scan. If you are using Square, make sure you have the app set up and bring your card reader.

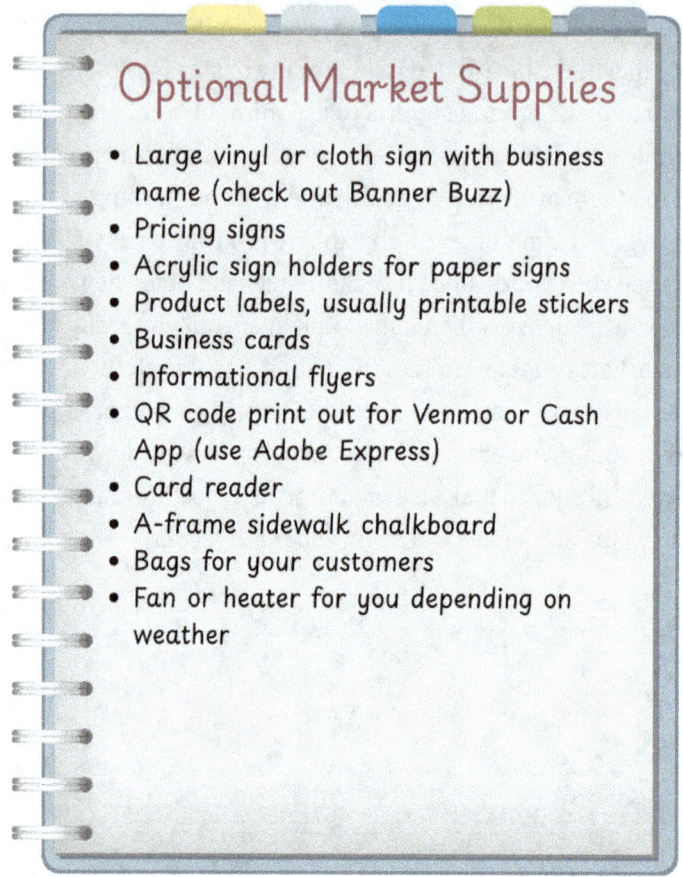

Optional Market Supplies

- Large vinyl or cloth sign with business name (check out Banner Buzz)
- Pricing signs
- Acrylic sign holders for paper signs
- Product labels, usually printable stickers
- Business cards
- Informational flyers
- QR code print out for Venmo or Cash App (use Adobe Express)
- Card reader
- A-frame sidewalk chalkboard
- Bags for your customers
- Fan or heater for you depending on weather

If you are a food vendor and sell food you bake, cook, or preserve yourself, you should look into the Texas Cottage Food Law. The cottage food law applies to small businesses selling less than $150,000 in product per year. This law explains what kind of foods you are allowed to produce and sell without needing a commercial kitchen. Generally, you are allowed to sell foods that don't require refrigeration and you are required to put a disclaimer on your products indicating that they were prepared in a home kitchen. You also need to list any allergens present in the food, such as milk or nuts. This website explains the law and how to write your labels. Just go to **texascottagefoodla w.com/sb541**. You can also check out the government website at **dshs.texa s.gov/retail-food-establishments/texas-cottage-food-production**. This website also allows you to apply for a registration number that you can list on your labels instead of listing your home address.

If you are selling non-food items, you'll likely need a Sales and Use Tax permit before you can sell. If you sell vegetables, fruits, or other food meant to be eaten at home you normally don't need to collect sales tax. See the chapter 8 on Sales Tax for more details.

My NoTes:

What markets in your area do you want to check out?

14

Vendor Stores

In some areas, you can find vendor stores that will let you rent a shelf and sell your items for you. This can be very convenient but your success does depend on the foot traffic of the specific store, as well as how high of a fee they charge you. But if you sell items that are shelf stable for at least a month or so, this can be a nice hands-off way to make sales.

To find a vendor store, you can start by doing a web search for "vendor store" and then visit them in person to see how they are set up and to talk to the owner. Ask about monthly fees and find out whether they take a percentage per sale. In some cases, they will take a percentage but will remit sales tax on your behalf.

To be successful in a vendor store, you'll want your items to fit the overall content of the store while still being unique and not duplicating any other products. You'll also want to create an inviting set-up with clear pricing signs and easy to understand information about your product. Many vendors include a bio to tell customers about themselves, or place a sign with their business name. You can usually also place your business cards or flyers on your shelf or store section.

To remain interesting to repeat customers, it will also be in your best interest to switch out products regularly and create new ones. If it fits your business, you can create seasonal products to attract customers. You can also do sales or specials, especially around the holidays.

Most store owners will be dedicated to your success and can help you build a successful display. Start with a small space, and as you become more successful, you can expand and put out more products. A single shelf is likely to be cheaper and will be easier to get started with. You can also still sell at markets or online even if you sell at a vendor store. But vendor stores can be a nice additional sales avenue.

If you sell produce or perishable items, farm stores are an option you can explore. Sometimes they will sell other vendor's products to supplement what they produce and give their customers more variety. You may need to visit these stores in person as well, and find out if they are already selling a similar product and if they accept products from outside vendors.

15

Selling From Home

Y ou might be wondering about the option of running your small business out of your home rather than selling at markets or vendor stores. Depending on what you're selling, you can offer pick up options or even set up a room or garage as a small store. Bakers especially seem to do well with home pick ups. If you have a lot of inventory, selling out of your home can also be easier since you won't have to transport all of your items. For example, plant growers may like to sell out of their garage or garden if they have a lot of inventory. The same can work for bakers or ceramics artists and others as well.

But the difficulty with selling from your home is that you lose some of your privacy, you need to be available to customers, and you need to bring customers to you. Having a large social media following can go a long way towards bringing in customers. Especially if you are selling something popular that people will travel for or may purchase often. Generally, that's why food businesses can do well when selling out of their home. If you can get repeat customers to buy from you regularly, selling from home may be successful for you.

Another way to get customers to come to you is to sell at markets or other locations and let customers know that you also offer pick up from your home. Hand out flyers to your customers and maybe offer additional varieties for home pick up than you do at market. If you often sell out of items at market, you can tell customers that if they order from you and pick up later, you can give them the items they want.

You can also post in Facebook groups as people often use them to look for local items to buy and small businesses to support. Fresh foods and bakery items can do well, as can eggs and other farm products. You may need to join several groups to see which ones will work best for you and get you the most responses. If your customers like what you provide, they may buy from you again and even tell their friends, which will bring in steady sales.

For most people I suggest starting with another option as well, such as markets. Selling from home only can be difficult when you're just getting started and it can be discouraging if sales aren't coming in. So selling from your home is easier to do once you have a customer base who is willing to come to you.

If you are renting your home, you need to consider one more thing as well. Most leases don't allow you to run a business out of the property. If you do, you may be in violation of your lease.

If you are running a service business, your home can work well as your place of business. Most service businesses either require you to travel to the customer's home or the customer to travel to your.

Hair, massage, or even pet grooming are some services that can be done out of a home. You can set up a room just the way you need it, and it's convenient for you. Most people are willing to travel for a service. You can also find businesses that complement yours and see if you can work together and share customers. For example, I often see pet day cares working with groomers to get their clients' dogs bathed and groomed. Something similar can work for you. This works especially well for pet-focused services. Pet sitters, trainers, groomers, and even pet treat bakers can share each other's information with their customers. Don't be afraid to reach out to other small businesses and support each other.

16

Social Media Sales

Creating a social media account is a useful way to share information with your customers. Most customers will be happy to follow you so that they can find out about new products and markets that you plan to attend.

I recommend that you choose one or two sites and create business profiles for them. Personally I like Facebook and Instagram for this, but it's up to you. While the younger generation may not be on Facebook much, it is still very popular with the customers you are trying to reach.

Once you've created your business accounts, write a short intro and start posting photos of you products and your creation process. Your followers will be interested to learn about you and how you create your items. While you may not have a lot of followers at first, they will grow over time. You can also use your personal account to invite people to follow your business page.

I also recommend that you use a QR code generator to make a QR code for your social media home page. Print it out and take it to markets with you. That way you can easily ask customers to follow you. Do be aware that some free QR codes expire and will stop working. I've found that Adobe Express is an easy to use, free version that can create QR codes that will not expire. Most customers will happily follow you if you ask.

Once you have your business social media pages, I suggest you use them to join local sales groups. Do a search for your city and see what groups exist.

This works mainly for Facebook. Join whichever groups you can and post your products or services. You can also post your products directly to Facebook marketplace. If you sell food, look for food or restaurant groups to join. If you sell crafts, look for craft sales groups. Some pages can only be joined by personal and not business accounts, so use your personal account as needed.

Keep posting regularly and over time, you will gain followers. Make sure your social media handles are listed on your flyers or business cards. List them on your website as well if you have one. If you join markets, post on their social media pages as well so that customers will learn about your products and come find you at market.

If you're a social media whiz, your account will likely take off in no time. But for the rest of us, having patience and just posting as you're able to will grow your followers over time. One way to make this easier is by creating and scheduling posts in advance. I like Publer for this because they have a free version with lots of features.

Also be sure to follow and like your fellow vendors' posts and social media accounts. They will likely follow you back and help you reach more customers.

Quick Tips & Info: Facebook URL CleanUP

Does the Facebook URL for your business page have a bunch of numbers at the end of it? Something like: www.facebook.com/pages/BusinessName/29475483 No worries! You can clean this up!
Click your profile photo in the corner, then **Settings and Privacy > Settings > Page Setup > Name** (in the app, click directly on **Username**). Then edit your **Username**. This will edit your link. Simplify it as much as possible and remove the numbers. (Make sure you edit your **Username**, not your **Name**)

17

Online Sales

N ow that you've set up your business, you'll need to decide if you want a website. Building a website is not hard and can be fun to do. But you don't necessarily need one. If you want to sell at markets and communicate with your customers through social media or email, you might be ok without a website. It really depends on how you want your business to work. If in-person sales or vendor store sales is all you want, then a website isn't required.

However, even some markets will ask for your website link if you have one, and it can help you get accepted into markets. But social media is enough in most cases. If you just want a simple website so that you can showcase your product and list the markets you sell at, that is perfectly fine. You can find free website options through Square, Wix, and similar sites. You'll want to create an About page, a page to display your product, and likely a contact page and calendar page to show your market dates. It doesn't have to be complicated.

If you want to sell through your website, you'll need to do a bit more work. You'll likely want a custom domain that corresponds only to your business, and you'll also need to add each of your products to your website's sale page. You'll need to decide if you will sell locally only, or if you will ship items to your customers. Look into shipping costs for your items' size and weight before you decide. Shopify is a good website builder for sales and shipping, and their cheapest plan starts at $29 monthly and includes a custom domain.

With a wide variety of plugins available, you'll be able to build a site that does pretty much anything you need it to. You can also offer home delivery to your customers and there are plugins that can help you set up delivery areas by zip code or distance. Allowing customers to pick up their orders at your home or at another location is another way to do it.

Once your site is ready, you can share it on your social media pages and at in-person markets. Having an active social media following will go a long way towards getting sales on your website. But you may still need to run advertising on Google or Facebook when you first get started. You should also make sure your website shows up on Google and other search engines. You can sign up for Google Analytics and Google Business Profile to help you set this up correctly. This will help you track your site's performance and create your business' profile on Google.

Getting reviews on Google or on your website will help a lot as well. Customers want to know that they can trust you and that your items are high-quality. If you can get your customers to leave reviews, you will have more success with online sales. Be sure to ask any of your in-person customers to leave reviews as well. Use QR codes that go directly to your review page to make this easier.

Building an email list is also a good way to reach your customers. You should have a sign-up form on your website, and if you can get people to join your list through social media that will really help you too. You can offer give-aways in exchange for sign-ups. Once you have an email list, you can send information on new products directly to your customers' inboxes. You can also tell them about in-person markets you might be at. And an email list is yours alone, it is not controlled by anyone else or subject to social media algorithms.

Selling through a secondary site like Etsy is another option. This way you don't need your own website, but you still need a page that draws customers in. You need a good product and you need people to see it. Etsy will also charge a fee for each item you post. Your success on Etsy depends a lot on how popular your niche is and how many other sellers are selling similar items. It can be hard to make it to the top of Etsy's search page, but you can also pay for Etsy advertising to help with this. You'll need to determine how to ship your items as well, so perishable items won't be a good option here. You can also do both and sell through Etsy as well as through your own website. This can give your product more exposure and increase sales.

While a website isn't necessary, even a simple one can help you share your product with customers and explain to them who you are. If you want to generate online sales then a more robust website with its own domain is going to help you be successful. If you aren't sure about online sales yet, you can always start with a simple site for now, or even leave website creation for later. In-person sales are often a more immediately successful option, especially for food items that can't be easily shipped.

18

Pricing Your Items

When pricing your items, you should take into account your sales location, cost of materials, overhead cost, and average pricing of similar items.

First, start your pricing on the higher side rather than the lower side. It is easier to go down in pricing than to go up, as your customers may notice and ask you about it. But, if you do find that your pricing is off, you can still go up if needed. Your customers know that you are running a small business and most will be understanding.

To get a general baseline, I suggest visiting nearby markets and seeing what similar vendors charge for their items. You can also search online to find out what a good price is, but this may not be as accurate for your area. And remember that you want to know what to price your handmade or home-grown item, not what a mass-produced version would cost.

You should also keep track of the supplies that go into making each item. You want to earn back more than you put in. You've put time, effort, and skill into your product. And you likely have other costs as well, such as driving to markets, website fees, advertising fees, and more. So never sell your items for less than the supplies that went into making them. Your current sales should allow you to purchase more supplies for future products, so you do need to make a bit of a profit. Think about how much you would be earning per hour of work that you've put into your products. What's a reasonable price when considering payment for your time?

Your sales location matters as well. People expect a certain price range based on the area. If you are selling at a small farmers market in a little town, you can't charge as much as you could in a wealthy city. If you are selling at a fair that only happens once or twice a year and has a high vendor fee, you can charge a bit more. People are there to enjoy a relatively rare event and will be ok with paying a bit more for a high-quality item.

When selling at markets, I like to take the market fee into account as well. If the fee is higher, I will charge a little more so that I can earn back the fee and a bit extra. But if the fee is low, I can charge a little less. For farmers markets, it is also better to price everything using whole dollars only. This makes it much easier to calculate change when people pay with cash. Increments of 50 cents are ok too but I wouldn't go any smaller than that for your and your customers' convenience.

So if your market charges a low fee and is in a small town, your customers will expect slightly lower prices than if you were selling downtown or in a larger city. Also think about the types of people who will be shopping at a particular market. Are they mainly retirees who are likely on a fixed income? Are they well-off? Did they travel far to come to this particular market and therefore are not as concerned with the price?

If you are selling your items at a vendor store, look at the over all price range of the store. Are items generally priced within a certain range? Are they priced higher than you would expect, or lower? What is the pricing of items most similar to yours? You can also ask the owner what they recommend as far as pricing. They should be able to tell you if your planned prices are reasonable. And of course, take into account your store fee as well.

Finally, see how your customers react to your prices. This works best when you're selling in person. Do visitors leave when they see the price? Do they comment on the price or seem surprised? Do they buy multiple items because your price is low? Do they suggest that you raise your price? You can also ask other vendors what they think of your pricing. They will likely be happy to help.

If you aren't selling in person, you will have to see if certain items sell and others don't, as well as how many items sell over time. If only your lower-priced items sell, then you may need to reduce the pricing of your other items. If items of a certain style or design sell, you need to adjust the design of your other items. And for those selling online, if you have a lot of website visitors but no one buys, your prices may be too high, or your website may need work to make it more attractive to customers. You can try a service like **uglybaby.io** which will review your website and tell you how to improve it.

If you are selling a service rather than physical items, your pricing strategy will be a bit different. You will need to focus more on the time spent on each service and the training or skills needed to be able to perform your service. You can look up similar businesses online for pricing ideas, and then increase your price for services performed at your customers' homes vs at your own home. Depending on your experience, you may also be able to charge more. If you are new, you can consider charging a little less until you get more experience. You can also charge extra for add-on services or a luxury service. And as with physical products, listen to your customers. Repeat customers are a great sign that your pricing is right on track. A lot of customers at once may be a sign that your prices are low.

Over time, your pricing strategy will improve. You will learn as you go along, and pricing is a little different for each niche. That's why looking at the prices of similar vendors is one of the best ways to come up with a good price. But be aware that some vendors also may not know how to price their product, so don't necessarily go with the highest or the lowest price you find.

What do you think is a good price for your items? Who do you want to sell to?

19

Final Considerations

N ow that your business is up and running, or will be soon, there are a few final thoughts I'd like to share with you to help you be successful.

Your Brand

What do you want people to think of when they see the name of your business? What do you want to show the world? What are the core values of your business? Do you want to build an environmentally sustainable business? Do you want to focus on handmade, one-of-a-kind items? Do you want to bring back skills that have been lost, such as weaving or blacksmithing? Do you want to give back to your community? How do you want to present yourself and your business out in public?

The colors and images you choose are important, as is your business name. Humor vs serious, cutesy vs bold, simple and straightforward vs unique and intricate. When you build a brand that stands for what you believe in, your business will be stronger and you will be happier. After all, you don't want to represent a business that doesn't embody your values.

While a lot of branding can happen online, it also happens every time you meet people at markets and every time someone sees how your items are displayed or packaged in a store. How you interact with customers matters as well. If they can hear your excitement and your dedication, they will be more likely to buy. If you are knowledgeable about your product and can answer a variety of questions, you'll build their trust and attract their interest. Friendliness is important too. Many market visitors will talk to you about your items but may not buy from you. But if you are friendly and welcoming they might buy from you another time.

Scheduling

Before you get too deeply into your business and every-day tasks, you should consider how flexible you want your life to be. If you sell at markets only, you can be quite flexible as far as taking time off or going on vacation. But if you sign customers up for weekly deliveries, it's much harder to take time off without notice. So consider how you want your business to function before you get drawn in and find yourself with commitments that you didn't plan for. Alternatively, maybe you prefer to do frequent deliveries instead of having to go to a market every week. And of course, you can combine as many sales locations and methods as you like and as fit into your schedule. Just make sure you know how busy you want to be before you get started!

The Future

What is your goal for your business? Do you want to grow and hire employees and maybe even step back eventually while your business maintains itself? Then you will likely want to form an LLC if you haven't done so yet. You'll also want to optimize your sales locations and only sell where you are most successful. Consider if you can reduce your costs by using different ingredients or changing packaging. Consider advertising to grow your business faster. If your earnings are high, you may want to file taxes as an S Corp to retain more of your profits. Once the workload increases and you have the funds, it might be time to hire employees. Most likely you'll want to find a professional to set this up for you or use an online service, as there are also several regulatory requirements such as reporting new hires to the government. Options like

onpay.com/payroll/software/costs-pricing will handle reporting, W-9 forms, employer taxes, and payments for you.

Is your goal to earn a small profit and mainly pursue your business to fund your hobby? Then you should prioritize your own enjoyment and avoid taking on too much. When something becomes an obligation rather than a choice, it can become less enjoyable. So step back when you need to. Attend as many markets as you want to, not as many as you can technically fit into your schedule. Do more of the parts you love and less of the parts that you don't. If you don't want to do social media, then don't do it. If you love social media but don't want to maintain a website, then don't make a website. If your business exists to bring you joy then focus on the aspects that will do that and build a business that brightens your life.

If your goal lies somewhere between these two options, then come up with a plan that works for you. If it's important to you to give back to your community, maybe you can donate money or some of the items you make. Write down your vision of what your business will look like in a few years and then work towards creating that vision.

About the Author

Helenna Snowden lives in Copperas Cove, TX with her husband, her dog, and her cat. She spends her free time growing and selling microgreens, and occasionally writing books. She also owns several rental houses together with her husband. She enjoys drinking tea and planting things. On weekends she sells at farmer's markets, spends time with family, and takes naps with her cat.